THE RECONSTRUCTION OF THE SPIRITUAL IDEAL

HIBBERT LECTURES, DELIVERED IN MAN-
CHESTER COLLEGE, OXFORD, MAY, 1923

BY

FELIX ADLER

"The Reconstruction of the Spiritual Ideal" by Felix Adler. ISBN 978-0-9897323-1-4.

Manufactured in the United States of America Printed in the United States of America

THE RECONSTRUCTION
OF THE SPIRITUAL IDEAL

Contents

THE RECONSTRUCTION OF THE SPIRITUAL IDEAL

I

DE PROFUNDIS

OUT of the depths into which it has fallen humanity cries to-day for help. But as yet there is no response. There seems in fact to be moral retrogression all along the line. The appalling number of divorces in all civilized countries indicates/the undermining of the family. The tension between employers of labor and wage earners is becoming more and more acute* Radical changes in the social order are contemplated. Profound changes of some sort seem inevitable, and can hardly be carried through without conflict. The horror of the recent war is still felt in our bones, and yet it seems as if mankind could not take to heart the most drastic lessons the most condign punishments. For alongside of the pacifistic current, preparations for new wars to be conducted by still more terrible methods are proceeding apace. Above all, there is one fact that strikes every observer: the so-called moral forces seem to have failed in the great crisis through which the world is passing. Religion was powerless to stay the carnage. Indeed, many of its representatives fell in with the prevailing fury, and on their part added fuel to the flames. Allah is said to have laughed aloud in his Mohammedan heaven when the news came that Christian preachers on the one side were proclaiming a Jehad or holy war against their Christian brethren on the other side. Again, the prayers for peace that were prescribed and recited in many churches were spoken into the wind; they had no effect on the combatants.

But already before these recent events moral ideals had fallen, at least among many of the intellectuals, into discredit. The followers of Marx openly sneered at what they called ideologies. Ethical ideals, in their opinion, are by-products or epiphenomena of the operation of economic factors. Economic considerations determine human history. At the same time it may be remarked that economic considerations had as little influence in preventing what happened as a moral considerations. The economists looked on as foolishly as did the moralists. The most irrefutable predictions of loss to the victor equally with the vanquished failed to cool the hot frenzy. Something more than the calculations of self-interest is needed to check the blood-lust,, to turn into safe channels the turbulent energies of human multitudes. The economist has no case in court against the moralist—both have failed in the crisis. Humanity cried loudly enough out of its depths, but neither had an adequate answer. Even now in the war that is being conducted after the peace, the common sense counsels of the best economists as well as of the moral idealists, are being swept aside with scant ceremony. But if we are to arrive at anything better than pessimism and discouragement, we had better make an end of complaints and turn our attention toward possibilities that promise results for the future. Immediately after the war the task of reconstructing human society was uppermost in people's minds. Extravagant hopes, tinged with millennialistic illusions, were to the fore. These hopes were doomed to prompt disappointment. But the task remains, as necessary, as urgent, as ever.

In this business of reconstruction, the economists, whatever their failures in the past, will have their part to play, and in regard to the proximate future perhaps the leading part. The statesmen also, if any exist—we scan the horizon eagerly to discern them—will have their part to play. But those who cannot get away from their worship of moral ideals will also have their part to play, and, looking to the far future, theirs will be the fundamental part. But they will have to go searchingly into the matter of the failure of the moral ideals in the crisis when humanity called out of the depths, and will have to ask themselves whether the ethical ideal failed because it was ethical, or perhaps because it was not ethical enough; whether it failed because it was ideal or because it was not comprehensively and profoundly ideal enough; whether, in short, the time has not come to reconstruct the moral ideal with: a view to giving it the power it lacks to grip men's wills and more adequately control their behavior.

I shall make an attempt in this book to sketch a reconstructed moral ideal, and test it by its applications to some of the most vital problems of modern life. But before taking up the subject, certain preliminary reflections may be in order.

An ideal is a thing desired, not yet realized. There are subjective and objective ideals. The subjective are in their nature private, the objective are public. The subjective correspond to desires which may be mere whimsies; the objective correspond to certain deep needs felt by many.[1]

Every great ideal is intended to be a relief from some sort of spiritual pain. Ideals are pang-born; they are the offspring of suffering; they are raised up before the mind in order to allay anguish. This is especially true of the religious or cosmic ideals. The history of religions might be written in terms of the particular types of inner pain which respectively they were designed to alleviate.

Goethe says somewhere: "When I suffer under the pressure of the finite I take refuge in the Infinite." Now the finite world presses upon men at different points, corresponding to the temperament of the people to which they belong, and to their development. Thus the Hindus were especially afflfcted by a sense of the unreality of things. To them the world seemed a vast phantasmagoria, the realm of *Maya,* or illusion; and

---

[1] This does not exclude that an objective ideal may at first be conceived by an individual; but then it must be of such a ⁻haracter as to spread, to be shared.

to escape the pervading consciousness of deception in things touched and seen, they formed for their relief the ideal of an abso-lute real, the one Brahma, a rock-bottom real, so to speak, a ground of things which would not dissipate into mist when handled —the mist of the veil of Maya. While the Buddhists in their turn, starting from the same conviction of the unreality of finite things, discovered, of thought that they had discovered, a remedy in the opposite direc-tion, the remedy being enlightenment as to the unreality of the soul itself which experi-ences the unreality of things. They cured the malady of the inner self by dissolving it in Nirvana. The two negatives combined as enlightenment constituted for them a sort of positive.[2]

The finite pressed upon the Consciousness of the Hebrew in a different Way, and at a different point. The Hindu was metaphysi-cal, the Hebrew was moral. The finite

---

[2] The above is given as my impression of Buddhism. I am not entitled to speak as a specialist.

world for the Hebrew was preeminently the human world. The pain that cut into his soul was the inversion of moral values as witnessed in this human world, the strong dealing ruthlessly with the weak, the oppressor on top,- the oppressed helpless under his heel. To the eye of the Hebrew prophet the fact of oppression was the one huge blot on the universe. The topsy-turveyness of the moral order was the one thing that excited those convulsive utterances that bear witness to the inner moral agony—the type of pain which the finite world as he saw it produced in him. He found relief by taking his flight toward the Infinite, by the ideal of a supremely righteous and omnipotent God, who in due time would redress the moral balance within the human sphere, give the earth and the fulness thereof to the righteous, converting or destroying the wicked.

In the Christian consciousness, Which at first was like the Hebrew, predominantly ethical, the metaphysical, Hellenic elements only entering later on, and even then as

ancillary rather than paramount, we encounter a new development. The Hebrews
always believed that the oppressor would
some time find his match. The yoke which
he rivetted on the necks of the oppressed
would definitely be broken; the triumph of
the good principle would be made manifest
in the victory of good men, those who embodied the good principle, over the bad men,
those who embodied the evil principle.[3] In
the Christian consciousness of those early
days, this blank dualism, this sharp distinction between the righteous and the wicked,
tended to be gradually modified. The ani-
mus of religious feeling was not so much
directed principally against the overtly
wicked, like the publicans, those shameless
exploiters, as against the stupidly self-right-
eous, who insisted on the pointed distinction
between themselves and the bad men. The
new development consisted in emphasizing the

---

[8] Somewhat in the same manner in which our naive con-
temporaries conceived of the victory of the Allies (the Czar of
Russia among the number) over the utterly bad Central
Powers.

same strain of evil present in the oppressed as in the oppressor, the same tendency to lust, anger and pride—in a word,
the type of pain in which the Christian religion took its rise was caused by the dis-
covery of the radical evil with which human
nature in general is afflicted.[4] And there was
a certain taking[1] sides with the oppressor, a
certain leaning toward him, a certain pity
and sorrow for his moral condition, and the
fine intuition that his experience might render him peculiarly fit to realize the crying
need of moral renovation.

Those writers who in our day endeavor
to represent Jesus as a kind of Socialist reformer seem quite to miss the purport of
His teaching. The Socialist says, wealth for
all; Jesus says, wealth for none. The difference is immense; the Socialist aims to abolish poverty, Jesus pronounces his beatitude
upon the poor. He does not sympathize the

---

[4] Which in the teaching of Jesus did not exclude the possibility of regeneration for all: "The Kingdom of Heaven
is within you."

less with those who endure oppression, yet
he blesses them when they are persecuted,
and suffer all manner of evil. The idea implied is that since the strain of wickedness
is in all men, the persecuted, who suffer
from its consequences, who feel in their own
flesh, so to speak, how the evil principle
hurts, shall use their experience to purge
their own nature of similar strains. This ex-
plains the doctrine of nonresistance, and
much besides.

It could not fail that pondering on this
universal presence of badness to the neglect
of the reassuring, confidence-giving affirmation, "The Kingdom of Heaven is within
you," should lead, among the less spiritu-
ally-minded followers of Jesus, to moral
pessimism, to absolute hopelessness, to a
sense of the utter depravity of human nature—and the relation of this to the appa-
ratus of orthodox Christian doctrine is plain.[5] In

---

[5]The Hebrew religion looked forward to the realization
of the moral ideal in a righteous community or state. When
the Jewish nationality was destroyed, the separate individuals
were left to seek salvation each in his own heart. This led
to excessive introspection, to the exaggerated importance

any case, the fact that a certain peculiar kind of inner pain was the starting-point of the Christian religion, and that there is a definite relation between this kind of pain and the shape which the Christian ideal took on, that there was a certain spiritual need, a profound affliction which some felt more acutely than others, but which was shared by many, and which constituted the objective basis of the ideal in its Christian form —this seems to me convincing.

I urge that in order to reconstruct society we must reconstruct the moral ideal. This is my main thesis which will be developed in various ways in the succeeding chapters. But we must have an objective basis for our ideal; and this we shall get if we make explicit to our minds the kind of spiritual pain by which we in the present age are chiefly afflicted. For often people are ill at ease, and yet are not clear as to what it is that troubles them, and cannot make their way through

---

ascribed to sex purity, and tended to corroborate and darken the pessimism referred to in the. text.

difficulties because they; have not sufficiently grasped the terms of the problems to be solved. Now as I reflect upon my own experience and upon the experience which others have communicated to me, it seems to me that the characteristic spiritual pain of our time is threefold.

First, the sense of the insignificance of man in this wide universe. The Psalmist confessed it plaintively despite his piety; Seneca states it eloquently, rhetorically; the eighteenth-century Montesquieu puts it, neatly. But never has the Lilliputian disparity between man and the magnitude of his world, the immensities of space, come home with such crushing force as it has to our own generation. A man six feet high is something of a giant in the eyes of his fellows. From the top of a moderately high hill he is no more conspicuous than a creeping ant. The earth, this junior planet on which we move about, seems a spacious realm to its inhabitants. We exult when, with the help of steam, or in airplanes, we "conquer distance." But what puny distance compared to that which separates us from the nearest fixed star! Geocentrism has been displaced by heliocentrism. Heliocentrism, in turn, the claim of the sun, surrounded by its satellites, to a sovereign place in the heavens, has become ridiculous in the face of the wilderness of suns that people the abysses beyond us. Astronomy, with every added perfection of its instruments, is revealing ever more and more those stellar, solar multitudes.

As with space, so with time. The geologic periods reduce the span of human life to a duration almost imperceptible. The ephemeridae live from morning to night— a single day is allotted to their existence. The day of a man, the vaunted threescore years and ten, is longer, but compared with the ages and the sons, is like the inhalation and exhalation of a breath* In every way, spatially and temporally, we are dwindling.

And not only as to quantity, but as to the quality of life, we seem to be losing caste.

Darwinism, the evolutionary theory, it would appear, administered the last stroke to our prerogative. The long procession *of* life-forms that has preceded us is unfolded to our vision. A humble place in the ranks is assigned to us. Is there any valid reason for supposing that we are more worth while than our predecessors?—insects, serpents, sheep and Oxen, the carnivorae. We do not claim for them an exalted significance in the scheme of things. They are products of nature, so are we. They have their noxious or kindly traits, so have we. They are waves of the flux, so are we. All our higher faculties, our mentality and our morality, is but the development of instincts "latent at the bottom of the scale of life; the highest out-reachings and aspirations we cherish, so we are told, are to be explained as outcroppings from below, no longer as apprehension of what is supremely above. Hume says, "In the sight of the universe, man is of no more account than an oyster." If Hume were living to-day, with what more drastic empha-

sis would he propound this depressing conclusion! Now a philosopher, placing himself in
his dispassionate survey on a level
with what is least considerable, may find a
kind of exaltation of himself in his very dis-
passionateness; but on the average man the
teachings of science fall like a pall, they are
a heavy weight under which his self-respect
endures an incurable depression. And note
that when men think meanly of themselves,
they are apt to act meanly; when men regard themselves as animals, they are apt to
behave as such.

Now no intelligent person will publish
himself an obscurantist and a fool by disput-
ing the teachings of science. The problem is
to extricate oneself from this heavy burden
that rests upon self-consciousness, without
stultifying the mind by subterfuges or eva-
sions. The truths of science must be received as such, but a way must also be found
of not only vindicating, but enhancing the
spiritual prerogative of man, of establishing
as a fact that there exists in him a spiritual

nature which exalts him, which gives him a unique place in the scheme of things. Seen from one point of view he is like Hume's oyster, or like oxen and sheep, a mere product of physical evolution; known from another point of view, he is far more than a development of the inferior life-forms. He is a witness of the infinite striking into the finite world. A reconstructed ethical ideal' must make good this proposition, must relieve mankind of the pain, the depression, due to profound self-depreciation and self-contempt.

The second mode of pain, which is felt far more acutely at present than at any other time, is due to the fate of those innumerable fellow beings who perish by the wayside, while mankind slowly and awkwardly tries to achieve progress—I mean those many thousands who are dying unhelped in the hospitals, I mean the victims of the foul conditions that exist in the slums, I mean the millions of young lives that were cut short during the late war. We stand, as it were, on the shore, and see multitudes of our fellow beings struggling in the water, stretching forth their arms, sinking, drowning, and we are powerless to assist them. We deceive ourselves as to the nature of the problem when we say that we will bend our energies to prevent others from perishing. That of course we are called upon to do by every spark of moral feeling. 'We must be incessant in our efforts to improve material conditions, but can we therefore avert our faces from the awful moral problem of those who perish in the meantime?

We have come to see a new relation be- [1] tween health, wealth, material goods generally and the spiritual nature of man, namely, the instrumental relation. The ascetics of all ages have said that material conditions are negligible; that wealth is a – thing indifferent, or even a hindrance. The secular-minded person of to-day looks upon wealth as an end in itself. The ethical point of views is that material goods are to be esteemed as ministerial to moral development, or to the manifestation of that worth which is latent in all men, and this implies that wealth is *only* to be esteemed in so far as it is ministerial to the higher development of man.

On this account we must be intolerant of bad material conditions, we must use our utmost efforts to abolish the foul slum, to encourage research into the causes and cure of disease. We must not flag in the war against war. And yet at the same time, here is the paradox in our inmost spirit, we must be patient of those very evils that will continue to endure, no one can say how long, and we must also exact patience of those who suffer the most. We are in the habit of saying "evolution not revolution," and we cannot help using such expressions, but we must be aware of what is involved in them, we may not shirk the issue. What is implied is that many will have to die without the health and wealth and education which we acknowledge to be instrumental to the development of the spiritual nature of men, before the necessary changes can be effected.

The forgotten man whom the social reformer is apt to overlook is the man who
perishes in the meanwhile, before the
schemes of social reform can even begin to
be adequately carried out. The social reformer is apt to live in his vision of the future, to feed on that' vision by way of anticipation, and to console those who are unhappy to-day by the prospect of happiness
to come. To be effective, however, this
method must represent the desirable changes
as proximate, and this is contrary to the slow
tempo inexorably prescribed by the facts of
mass psychology. Or, if this method is
avoided, if the social reformer is of a gentle
type* not "scientific" in the fashion of the
Marxists, if he shrinks from cutting the Gor-
dian knot, he will have to fall back on sympathy as a means of making those who suffer
in the meantime contented with their lot, assuming, as then he must, that the sunny picture of universal happiness in the next generation, or the next after the next, will cast a

reflected gladness into the hearts of those who threaten to sink under the heavy burdens which they bear at present. But sympathy depends on a vivid imagination, which is usually the gift of the reformers themselves, but hardly of the generality of mankind. Again, sympathy is intermittent in its action, flowing and ebbing; and sympathy, so far as it calls upon men to sacrifice the happiness of those who live to-day to those who will live later on, is inconsistent with the ethical doctrine of the equal worth of all human beings. Why should I be a mere stepping stone over which the crowd is to pass to its earthy Elysium?

Moreover, there is a distinction between extensive and intensive sympathy. The former extends over the indiscriminate mass, embraces in a vague way humanity in general. It is wide but shallow, easily kindled into enthusiasm, but, save in exceptional individuals, not a constant driving force. The latter, the intensive sympathy, fastens upon near objects, on friend and brother, wife and child; and when it happens that one of these near and dear objects is about to perish in the meantime, this intensive sympathy resents and rebels against any form of consolation dependent on the sacrifice of the present to the future. The mother who sees her child succumbing to a disease which medical science has not conquered, will ask: Why should my child die in order that others may live? Why should this dear head become dust in order that other people's children may grow up happy? No, sympathy does not by any means meet the painful problem which I am emphasizing. Marcus Aurelius justly said: "It is possible to be a man, even in a palace"; and we may and must say that it is possible for a man to be a man even in the slums. Yes, this is not only a possibility, but an actuality. Many a man, many a woman especially, exemplifies the dignity of human nature amid the most repellent conditions. We must therefore proceed in both directions. We must sharpen the effort to improve those conditions which are instrumental to the development of the moral nature of man. There must be no relaxtion, no lying down under the difficulties that bar the way, and at the same time we must vindicate the present worth which is independent of ccnditions. The spiritual ideal must meet both these requirements. And let me say, in concluding my remarks on this point, that the problem of those who perish in the meantime will never cease to exist. For let poverty be no more, let disease be abolished (although we are told by medical authorities of new diseases that are appearing, diseases of civilization), let all the grosser, more palpable evils of society be removed—yet, m the ^progress of science, and in the more complex adjustments of human beings to one another, as the idiosyncrasies of individuals become more pronounced, there will always be those who are unequal to the new tasks imposed and to the gains achieved by the more advanced, and who, in a certain sense, will perish in the meantime. The grosser problems with which mankind still has to deal are in a way a screen that hides the finer, more subtle, and certainly not less painful problems which will face mankind hereafter.

The third problem is constituted by the need of relief from the, intolerable strain of the divided conscience. *"A* house divided against itself cannot, stand human nature in revolt against itself cannot rest. By the divided conscience I, do not mean what is sometimes called the departmentalized conscience, or the arrangement, so to speak, of water-tight compartments in the inner life. Of that indeed we see many examples, as in the case of persons who are fine and even exquisite in their private relations, but are hard as nails in business, unscrupulous partisans in politics, or lying diplomatists for their country's supposed good. But the intolerable strain of. the divided conscience of which I speak is felt by men who are eagerly desirous to make their life whole, all of a piece, of achieving consistency in their conduct throughout, and who do not see how

to do it because they find that the ethical
standard which they acknowledge in their
private relations, and which they /would like
to expand so as to cover their business and
professional relations, their conduct as citizens, is incapable of such expansion. In
other words, they have a moral standard to
hold to when they deal as individuals with
other individuals, but find themselves destitute of any sufficient moral standard to guide
them where they are required to act as members of groups.[6] The absence of a standard
regulating the morality of groups is to-day
the great, the crying defect. The family is
one such group; the duties of the man toward
the woman and of the woman toward the
man, of the two adults toward their children,
cannot be governed on the private; moral
standard furnished by the Golden Rule.
That rule says: Put yourselves in the other's

---

[6] A man engaged in large business transactions approached
a Christian clergyman of my acquaintance "with this request
'"Can you tell me how I can lead the Christian life in business?"*'
and the clergyman confided to me that he had 'found it difficult
to give a satisfactory answer. Difficult—I reflected—on
Christian premises, is it possible?

place, and then in imagination deicide upon the other's rights according to the claims which you yourself would feel justified in making. The Golden Rule assumes that the parties concerned are related as like to like. Hence the imaginary transposition of oneself into the other's place decides what is right. But men and women are unlike, adults and children are unlike, the claims and obligations on either side are unlike. The various vocations—agricultural, industrial, commercial, professional—are exercised in groups. The relations within these groups are those of the unlike to the unlike. So are nations groups; and it is just a morality of groups, both an internal morality, that of the members of the groups to one another, and an external morality, that of the groups to other groups—it is just this immense need of a morality of groups that has not been met. Where there should be definite standards there are none; where there should be ideals of behavior there is a void.

I submit that the reconstruction of the moral ideal is indispensable as a basis for the reconstruction of society. It is the necessity of working out the morality of groups that makes this task of reconstruction from the practical point of view so incontestably urgent, and it is to this task that I shall endeavor to contribute in the chapters on "Permanence and Impermanence in Marriage," on "The Ideal of Social Reconstruction," on "The State and International Relations."

To what has been said I wish to subjoin three points.

1. The reconstruction of the moral ideal does not mean merely extending the field covered by the ethical principle... It does not mean merely adding new ethical provinces, such as business morality, political morality, international morality to the province of private morality already covered. The same ethical principle must run like a golden thread through all human relations, and the new applications in the wider group relations

will inevitably react upon the morality of the private life, correcting and deepening it. Thus the moral attitude toward the sense part of man, the moral attitude toward wealth, the moral attitude in respect to nonresistance, as enjoined by the traditional private morality, will be profoundly modified by the attempt to discover a rule of conduct embracing the public as well as the private life. Business ethics, political ethics, and international ethics will be found in many ways to transform private ethics.

2. In default of an ethical principle to govern the relations of groups to one another, since the social order depends upon the adoption of some principle governing the relation of groups, history shows that one dominant group has invariably subordinated and oppressed the others. And that group dominated which exercised the particular function at any one time esteemed the most distinguished. Thus the sacerdotal function as exercised by the Brahmins was esteemed in India the most distinguished, that

in which the excellence of-human nature was
most manifest (for the Brahmin was powerful enough to compel the gods themselves to
do his bidding) and in consequence the
arrangement of the social groups was based
on the predominance of the Brahmin priest-
hood. Under the feudal constitution of society the exercise of the military function
was most esteemed. In capitalistic society
the function of wealth accumulation domi-
nates. Some one function hitherto has always been ranked above the rest, and the social groups have been-ranked hierarchically
accordingly. The ethical problem, the real
problem, for instance, of what we call democracy is, to place all functions on a level with
respect to the worth of those who exercise
them, and to propound a spiritual ideal in
which this equality may be realized, not despite the inequalities, but by their interaction.

3. Plato, the philosopher, was of the opinion that the ills of society would be cured if
only the philosophers could be induced, how-

ever reluctantly, to become rulers. I have often asked myself, in attending philosophic congresses or listening to the discussions in philosophic clubs; what would happen if these our modern philosophers were invited to undertake the office which Plato would assign to them. I do not intend here to indulge in cheap innuendo against philosophy. Philosophic speculation has had and still has its high uses. The brave attempt to embrace in one synoptic view the lofty problems of the mind is bracing even where it fails, and besides, each of the great systems has been stimulating outside its field in the sciences and arts. Iron-clad agreement is not the ultimate test. Disagreement also has its value. But just in the field of ethics the outcome of speculation has been gravely disappointing, and the reason, I take it, is that the prime interest of philosophers as a rule has been scientific or logical, or perhaps aesthetic, not ethical; and on this account they have approached the problems of ethics with ruling concepts derived from their preoccupation with physical science, or biology, or aesthetics, and have then endeavored to fit the data of ethics into a scheme derived from data outside the field of ethics. In Aristotle's philosophy the dianoetic virtues tower high above the ethical. In Kant, the Newtonian physics shines through the Categorical Imperative, however sublimely proclaimed; in Hegel the dialectic process determines his reasoning on moral as well as other questions.

Is it not possible to take a new turn in ethical philosophy, to insist that ethical theory shall be based primarily upon ethical data, and shall aim directly, and not by way of circumlocution, at the solution of the distinctly ethical problem?—and by the ethical problem I mean that of reconciling the individual sacred as an end *per se* to other individuals no less sacred than himself. It is true that the Hebrew and Christian religions have built on this foundation, but their ideals contain a large admixture of mythological and other elements derived from nonethical sources. Is it not possible to have a pure ethical ideal? Cannot a theory be proposed —for a theory of some sort we must have; the regulation of conduct cannot be left to mere instinct or sentiment—which shall consult the ethical data exclusively to begin with, shall seek to fit itself to these data, and not the data to itself, and which shall still be subject to revision as ethical data accumulate, as ethical experience widens and deepens?

II

THE SPIRITUAL IDEAL

THAT an ideal, in order to be objective, must correspond to certain deep-felt needs has been set forth in the previous chapter. The correspondence is required, but on what principle shall the ideal be framed so as to meet this requirement? How shall we go about effecting the necessary changes in the ideal?

The thesis of the present chapter is that the spiritual ideal takes one shape or another according to the way in which the spiritual nature is defined. In brief, the spiritual ideal was originally gained by defining the spiritual nature in a certain way. This original definition is found in the Hebrew religion. The spiritual ideal was then reconstructed—that is exactly the word to be used —in a second act of definition. Two stages of definition have been passed, a third, a new reconstruction, now awaits us. In the Hebrew religion the spiritual part of man was conceived under the attribute "holy." The spiritual nature is a holy thing. Now the primary meaning of holy is aloof, separate; a holy being is one who keeps himself separate, who is inaccessible within his precinct, whom it is perilous to approach too closely, who resents and punishes trespass on the territory he occupies. The sentiment inspired by such a conception is one of awe: "Take off thy shoes from off thy feet, for the place whereon thou standest is holy ground."

The Hebrews defined the spiritual nature of man by circumscription of its sphere, by the delimitation of its frontiers, and the chief ethical rule derived was—Thou shalt not trespass, not on the life, not on the property, not on the reputation of another; thou shalt not invade, thou shalt not encroach, for holiness does not permit encroachment or invasion.

The Hebrew did not venture to examine the spiritual nature *per se,* he stood too much in dread of it, in awe of it. The spiritual nature of man is like the spiritual na-. ture of God, the latter merely raising the former to the the degree. A similar attitude as to the Holy One of Israel is prescribed toward man. "Thou canst not see His face and live - neither can anyone really penetrate the inner sanctuary, the soul of man, nor see a shape within the inner sanctuary of the soul of man. It is a significant fact that stories of ghosts or apparitions are almost absent in the Old Testament. At any rate the spiritual was not conceived of as ghostly by the teachers of the Hebrew religion, and necromancy, which attempts to come- into communication with the dead, that is, to deal with ghosts, was especially abhorrent to the prophetic writers.

It is true to say that the Hebrew religion conceived of the spiritual nature of man ethically, but we should always be on our guard against injecting into such words as "ethical," a modern modification of meaning. "Ethical" in general refers to the way in which a man ought to behave to his fellowmen, the way in which it is right that he should behave. But there are all sorts of opinions as to how a man ought to behave. And therefore to say that the spiritual nature was conceived as ethical by the Hebrews is not sufficiently descriptive. Rather their ethics was derived from their conception of the spiritual nature. The right way to behave, according to them, was to honor in one's conduct the holy presence in human beings, and to honor it more particularly by not invading their personality, or encroaching upon it. Hence the conspicuous place occupied by the idea of justice in the ethics of the Hebrews.[1] Justice with them meant essentially the awe-inspired respect

---

[1] Justice, too, is a general term that covers many diverse meanings. For instance, in Plato's *Republic* it connotes an arrangement by which every human peg is put into its appropriate hole. It is an attribute pertaining to a hierarchical arrangement of society in which the inequalities of human nature are stressed, whereas in the Hebrew conception of justice the equality is stressed.

for the personality of others; and since oppression is a most flagrant manifestation of
disrespect for the personality of others, the
oppressor is marked throughout the Hebrew
Scriptures as the typical enemy of the holiness idea, and the final disappearance of oppression is represented as synonymous with
the realization of justice, and as the goal of
the history of mankind. A too narrow view
of justice, one might say, from the modern
point of view, but immensely valuable and
true as far as it goes.[2]

The holiness idea, I repeat, is thus to be
regarded as furnishing the ruling principle
in this ethical scheme. Justice is the first
and chief practical corollary derived from it.
Do not violate the rights of others, such
rights being due to the holy presence in
them. Mercy and humility are the two other
practical corollaries. "For what doth the

---

[2] Note the difference between the above and the *nolle me
tangere* formula of Mill, the liberty of the individual within
the limits of noninterference with the liberty of others. In the
one case you have liberty a purely naturalistic attribute, in
the other case you have a spiritual attribute.

Lord require of thee, but to do justly, and to love mercy, and to walk humbly with thy God?" The ever-recurrent examples of mercy are, care for widows and orphans, that is, protection of the unprotected, of those who are destitute of the physical force to make good their rights—rights which in their case also are due to the holy presence inhabiting them. It is evident that the greater the personal dignity we astribe to human beings, the more unendurable will it be to see such a one reduced to the last extremities of indigence and suffering. The feeling thus aroused is similar to that ex-cited when we behold the scion of a noble house reduced to beggary, or a king's son in rags. Every human being, in virtue of the spiritual or holy nature is, as it were, clothed with something of the attribute of sover-eignty and the sight of such a being in ex-treme indigence evokes the kind of feeling denoted by the Hebrew conception of mercy. Humility again is induced by the sense of one's failure to live up to the acknowledged standard of conduct, and by an estimate of the distance that separates man from his own supreme ideal of holiness. '

There are other more subtle developments of the Hebrew ethics, for instance, the idea of the vicarious, expiatory suffering of the innocent (Isaiah liii) namely, the suffering of Israel for the salvation of those peoples of the earth who have not won the same insight into the holiness ideal acknowledged by Israel. But it is unnecessary here to follow this evolution of the Hebrew thought. The main point I am setting forth is that the Hebrew ideal was shaped according to a certain method, namely, by a definition of the spiritual nature, that the Hebrews did not attempt to define that nature as it is in itself, but defined, its frontiers, and that in the main, in an. initial thrust at all events, the practical rules of conduct are summarized in the dictum "Thou shall not trespass."

In the second, the Christian stage, definition went a step farther. The territory of the inner life was boldly entered. The awful sense of aloofness had to some extent diminished, and a bifurcation was attempted within the inner man. The holy thing in him was separated off by a sharper distinction between it and the things in him that are not holy, such as appetite, anger, pas sion, pride—"He who looketh upon a woman with an unclean eye hath already committed adultery in his heart," etc.; "Leave there thy gift before the altar;" "If anyone compel thee to go with him a mile, go with him twain." The problem had taken a new turn. It was no longer the holy people but the holy individual that constituted the chief object of concern. For the national state had fallen into ruins, and the individual was to work out his spiritual destiny no longer as included in an ideally just community, but standing on his own feet, remitted to his own resources —just a man, loose from the national connections, no longer leaning on public law, but dependent on his own effort, or, if that should fail him, as soon became apparent, on the personal assistance of a superhuman, divine individual.

What concerns us here for our purpose is the change in the spiritual ideal brought about by the new step taken, in definition. The ideal of holiness remains. ; But holiness is no longer primarily manifested in justice, and the like, in action, in one's relation to others. It is primarily manifested in that which takes place within the man himself. The holy thing "is defined by contrast with the unholy things in a man; and holiness consists in segregating the holy nature from the unholy, in extricating the spirit from its entanglement with appetites, passion and pride. The spiritual nature of man is thus defined by way of negation. It is that which is not of the world, the flesh, or of the principle of darkness, which is not our worldly nature, carnal nature, obscurely evil nature. And if justice is the ruling concept in the Hebrew ethics, then purity, in the sense of freedom from admixture, is the ruling concept in this earliest type of the Christian ethics..

But there is also a positive connotation to this new; definition, for freedom from admixture implies a substantive something which repels foreign elements, which seeks to maintain its unbroken integrity,, its self-identity. The spiritual nature is thus conceived as unitary, as self-identical. It is engaged, during its finite experience, in resisting those influences which seek to drag it away from its own ground, to induce self-alienation, or departure from itself. The metaphysical idea latent in the Christian ethic—and a metaphysical idea of some sort is latent in every ethical system—is that of self-conservation, self-affirmation, "self" meaning an indefeasible, unitary entity.

But man is only too well aware of his frequent departure from this high, self-resting posture, is only too often reminded of the concessions he makes to his worldly, carnal, and obscurely evil nature. Life, therefore, is a kind of moral agony, an incessant combat against attacking forces! and this conflict is only terminable, the agony is only

pacified, when the unitary self sets its face'
unyieldingly toward the supreme One, the
divine ideal of unity in whom there is no
change nor shadow of turning.

For man, the earthly pilgrim, there is a *terminus a quo* and a *terminus ad quem.* The
terminus a quo is the manifold, not only the
manifold of the senses, but also the manifold
of this picturesque world so far as it ex-
cites intellectual curiosity. For science, too,
and the pursuit of profane knowledge, is to
be shunned as drawing the soul away from
its centre ("Blessed are the poor in spirit").
And the *terminus ad quem* is God the One.

I have pointed put the negative and the
positive aspects of the spiritual nature as
defined in the Christian ethic; the social aspect of it is no less subtly significant. This
was expressed in the development undergone
by the Hebrew idea of mercy in the Christian idea of love. There was a note of tenderness in the Hebrew idea of mercy. This
received a newly nuanced mellowness in
Christian love. Individualism, I reassert,

was the starting-point. The Christian was concerned with the distinction between the holy thing and the unholy things in himself, but every individual Soul was or might be a temple of the Holy Ghost, was inhabited by the same holy presence. Every human being was or might be a pilgrim journeying from the *terminus a quo* to the *terminus ad quern,* from the world of the manifold toward the infinite One. Now love, primarily, was the sense of companionship with others who are journeying on the same road, arid a feeling of keen desire to help them on the way. Hence the chief expression of Christian love always has been and is the promulgation of the faith, since it is impossible to render a greater service to any fellow-being than to promote his reaching the ultimate goal. This was the real charity or *caritas,* and if charity also took on its-more palpable forms, of feeding the hungry, visiting the sick and the like, such acts of charity were symbolic rather than pragmatic in object. They resembled the offering of a flower to a beloved

person, a tribute to his preciousness, rather
than a gift valued for its material use. If
the young man was directed by Jesus to sell
all that he had and give it to the poor, it was
not intended that he should confer wealth
on the poor, which would have been a contradiction in terms, but that he should manifest both his own independence of wealth
and his appreciation of the personality of
those whose extreme indigence he relieved.

One might say God is the spiritual sun,
and every human soul a ray of that sun.
The destiny of each individual is to travel
along the line of that ray, backward, upward, toward the central light. And love
is the sense of latent luminousness in all our
fellow pilgrims. Love is the sense of indi-
rect union with them (by a detour, as it
were) by way of the common focus of all our
natures—only that this simile might suggest
a pantheistic construction of the relations of
men to the Deity. And while undoubtedly there
was a pantheistic strain in the Christian; consciousness, as when Paul speaks of

the time when God shall be all in all, yet actual pantheism was prevented by the ethical conception of man. For, despite his relations to God, he is still somehow *qua* ethical, an independent being, responsible for his acts, so that though the company of spirits yearns‑ towards God, travels Onward toward God, they are never merged with God, submerged in God, their final destiny being pictured as that of a company of souls surrounding the supreme spirit, dwelling in the light of his presence.

A third step in the definition of the spiritual nature is now required. The situation in which the world finds itself demands it. The historical situation, and the needs in it as felt by ethically sensitive minds, is ever the challenge that provokes the construction or reconstruction of the spiritual ideal. Not that the historical situation is the cause, it is the evocative occasion. Thus the black fact of oppression was the challenge that provoked the Hebrew ideal of justice. "Woe to them who add land to land, that grind the faces of the poor, etc." The forsakenness of the individual when the national state failed as a moral support, the return of the individual upon himself, as described above, evoked the Christian ideal. And the triple need of our own generation, as set forth in the first lecture, more particularly the need of a group morality, is the challenge to those who are ethically sensitive for the formation, the reformation, the reconstruction of a spiritual ideal that shall be apt to respond to the need. How shall this be produced?

I have already said it—by definition, by a stricter definition, by coming to closer quarters with the spiritual nature, taking hold of it mentally with a firmer grasp.

We need a morality of groups. The groups are the family, the vocational group, the, state, the nations comprised within the international society. Each group consists of, is constituted by, unlike individuals exercising unlike functions. The unlikeness of function is the mark that distinguishes a group from a herd. In the family the dis-

similarity is that of the two sexes, the dissimilarity of age, of the adults and their offspring. In the vocational groups the dissimilarity is that of talents. In the state the
dissimilarity is that of the agricultural, industrial, commercial, professional groups,
fulfilling different types of social service. In
the international group the dissimilarity is
that of the various types of civilization represented by the different peoples. As will
be seen, the desirable relations within the
groups, and of the groups to one another,
is what is commonly called organic. But
this word organic must be subjected to an
extremely careful inspection. An organism
is described as a whole the parts of which
are mutually dependent in such sort that
each part or member in the fulfillment of its
distinctive function conditions the discharge
of function by the rest, and is in turn con-
ditioned in the fulfillment of its function by the
rest.[3] In this sense the whole is present

---

[3] The cause and effect interpenetrate. That which is cause is at the
same time effect, and that which is effect is simultaneously cause.

in each part, and each part indispensable to the whole. But where can such an organism be found—an example that corresponds to the idea of such a necessary relation of parts to one another as is implied in the definition? For the relation, note well, must be a necessary one; each member in functioning must be the indispensable condition of the functioning of the rest —otherwise the relation is fortuitous, and not truly one of interdependence. The animal body is not an example, though it is superficially, vulgarly used as such. There are in it rudimentary parts. The cooperation of the different parts is imperfect. Of the five senses we cannot say that they are necessary, such as they are, that more perfect instruments would not be conceivable, or that the addition of a sixth or seventh sense would not. facilitate the smooth working of the others, and prolong the body's existence. Finally the absence of necessity in that physical system which we call the body is demonstrated beyond dispute by its fatal, inescapable dissolution, by the fragility of the coherence of its parts. If the coherence were necessary it could not cease. That is "necessary" the nonexistence of which is unthinkable.

If, then, there is no actual example of an organism, if what we see in plants and animals, and still more imperfectly in human society, are adumbrations of an idea which we carry in the mind, not drawn from external experience, but applied to it as a standard, how does it arise in the mind? The two polar conceptions in the mind are that of unity and that of plurality. There have been many attempts in the history of philosophy to ignore one of these polar concepts, in consequence of a predilection for the other. There have been monistic systems and pluralistic systems, vain attempts to exhibit how difference can be drawn out of the bosom of unity; futile attempts to show how unity can be wrought out of sheer pluralities. The truth is that unity and plurality are two blades of a pair of shears, and that one can cut with neither singly; that one can derive neither from the other, the mind being constrained to use them jointly. It is this joint use that has led to every actual gain in knowledge. It is this joint use on which the progress of mankind in the quest of objective reality depends. Ever there must be singled out some 'manifold which shall be at the same time comprehended as a unity. But whatever manifold is given in experience, such as the manifold of space in geometry, the manifold of sequence in physics, etc., is ever incomplete, partial, and on this account the fundamental impulse of the mind toward the unification of manifoldness, toward the complete interpretation of the two polar concepts, can never be satisfied. There is ever a surplus of plurality not embraced, the total field is never covered, the task remains exasperatingly unachieved.

Now the ideal of a system such as is denoted by the word 'organism" is nothing else than the ideal produced by the mind of the complete use of the two polar concepts.

It is the ideal of a plurality infinite in quantity, the parts of which are infinitely diverse in quality, while at the same time the relation between them is a necessary one, that is to say that the nonexistence of any one of the infinite diverse parts is unthinkable. Each in its place is indispensable to the whole, the whole in its effect is indispensable to each. The organic ideal thus conceived is the outgrowth of the search of the mind for objective reality. The objectively real is that which is necessarily actual. The mind's search has led it beyond finite experience into transcendental regions. There in the transcendental the mind plants its uttermost conception of objective reality.

But you will say that all this construction is metaphysical, and what is its bearing on the problems of group morality? What has it to do with the cry *de profundis*—with the disorders of the world and the problems of social reconstruction? There is a certain metaphysic, as I have already observed, underlying every ethic. It is usually latent.

There are metaphysical powers that work in what the Freudians call the *subconscious,* even in the case of those who are least aware of them, and there is gain in exposing them, at least to the metaphysically inclined. For the average man, and even for the metaphysician himself, however, it is not the abstraction, but the force which penetrates into consciousness, that works, that moves, that influences. And in the case of the subject with which we are dealing it is ethical experience, certain facts of moral consciousness, that give vitality to what might otherwise seem shadowy.

The fact of moral consciousness that counts above all others is the judgment that man is an end *per se.* To say end *per se* is to attribute to him worth. In this form we retain the Hebrew concept of holiness. Holiness equals end *per se.* But worth must be distinguished from value, and this distinction is of the most far-reaching importance.

Value is a relative term—relative to him or to those who evaluate. If he or those who evaluate were to disappear, value would disappear. But to say worth, or end *per se,* is to make a cosmic pronouncement, is to affirm of man, that is, of the spiritual nature of man, a preciousness that would remain though all the finite world, and all the finite beings that inhabit it were swept away. To say end *per se,* or worth, of man is to place him (so far as his spiritual nature is concerned) as a member in that infinite plurality infinitely unified, the *corpus spirituals,* the infinite organism, of which I have spoken. So far as he is regarded as a member of that, he is indispensable; because of his spiritual nature his life, his property, his reputation, are to be held inviolate. He is not to be slain as oxen and sheep are slaughtered; he is not to be enslaved, he is not to be employed as a mere means to any finite ends of his fellows. His reputation, for instance, is not to be jeopardized to minister to the vanity or pride of his fellows. And all this, not because the human creature as a product of physical nature is deserving of reverence, but because there is a holy thing in him, however feebly it shines through him. The Hebrew holiness is now defined as worth; the Christian principle of self-identity, the irreducible intactness of the spiritual part of man, is also retained but modified, so that to speak metaphorically, there shall not be conceived the same Christ in all, but so that the divine principle shall be conceived as having a different face in each. For it is the unlikeness that is the foundation of the reconstructed ethical ideal, the unlikeness of the functionary in the infinite *corpus spirituale.* It is this unlikeness that makes him indispensable, and the being indispensable is the essence of his moral character.

But one more step needs to be taken. We speak no more of the God of Hosts, but, as it were, of the host as godhead. We speak of an infinite society, an infinite choir, a commonwealth of spiritual beings, each of which expresses the spiritual nature in a manner unlike all the rest. And this unlikeness,

it must be insisted again, is irreducible.
The integrity of each member is imperme-
able. How then can the host become a system? How can the unity of so vast a multitude of beings be conceived, each one of
which, in the intimacy of his unlikeness,
seems inaccessible to the rest. The unity is
predicable only in the form that the unlikeness of each is such as to elicit the unlikeness in all the rest. And from the scheme of
relations thus conceived, there is .derived a
new vital practical ethical rule/Seek to
elicit the best in others, and thereby you will
bring to light the best that is in yourself;
evoke, the distinctive unlikeness of others,
and thereby you will promote and produce
the destructive unlikeness which is your own
essential self. Seek to educe in the other the
consciousness of his indispensableness, that
is, of his membership in the infinite spiritual
commonwealth, and in so doing you will gain the
conviction of your own membership
therein. You will not *save* your soul, but
achieve the unshakeable conviction that you

are soul, or spirit.

The spiritual nature is now defined, first as holy in the sense of worth; second as ir-reducible, in the sense of uniqueness, thirdly as organic.[4]

---

[4] The individualistic ethic, with its individualistic concep-tion of divinity, involves that the perfection of infinite being exists, and has existed from all eternity in the one God. If this be so, man's existence is superfluous. He is at best an imperfect copy of the divine model. And why should such im-perfect copies as he and his fellows exist at all? He is an afterthought; he is not indispensable. But this is contrary to the ethical judgment of worth, meaning indispensableness. The infinite ideal, as sketched above, places man within the circle of godhead, where he belongs. He is no longer an out-lander, but a citizen.

The empirical ethical systems, shrinking from metaphysical speculation, as too abstract, and seeking to discover concrete ground on which to build, have recourse to what appear to be palpable traits in human nature such as appeal to common sense. The two traits chiefly singled out are selfishness and sympathy. There are egoistic systems' of ethics and altruistic systems. Sidgwick perplexed his mind without success to find a bridge between the two; but it suffices here to say that the sure ground upon which these systems are built turns out to be the least sure, and that in any case no proper ethical judgment can be founded on either. -

The error in supposing that the palpable is the sure is being increasingly discredited in the domain of science. Helmholtz described the force or energy with which the physicist deals, as a thing in itself incognisable and unimaginable, known, how-ever, in its measurable effects. This he laid down as against-Goethe, who, in his Theory of Color, impatient of the un-imaginable, had insisted that the ultimates of potential visibility should be taken as. the last terms of- permissible scientific speculation. Helmholtz's definition of force comes very near the notion of a metaphysical entity unknown in itself, but known in and through its effects.

In the above sketch of the spiritual ideal, I have indicated the way to advance in the theory of ethics where .we are dealing with far subtler energies than in physics, beyond the palpabili-

The; ethical rule, derived from the spiritual ideal, furnishes the morality of groups, both internally, and in the relation of groups to one another. Let the unlike seek to elicit the unlike, but always under the condition and with the proviso that the unlike is not the merely original, but rather that dissimilarity which is prolific of new dissimilarity, and which in action and reaction evokes in the participants the consciousness of the infinite spread of the ideal of the manifold.

In each group there is supplied some natural, some empirical motive, favorable to the application of the spiritual rule, the substratum, as it were, of the spiritual relation within that group. In the family it is the attraction of the sexes and the parental instinct. In the vocational group it is a certain initial interdependence never complete between the different functionaries in respect to their diverse gifts and talents. Similarly in

---

ties of egotism and sympathy. In ethics also are, to be recognised sources of energy, centralities of spiritual energy, points of luminousness unimaginable in themselves, but *known in* their effects.

the state it is the initial and partial interdependence of the vocational groups upon one another. In the international society it is the partial initial dependence for mutual supplementation of the different types of civilization represented by the different peoples. The morality of the groups consists in the spiritualizing of the given, natural substratum, and in the attempt to carry out this task of spiritualisation the reality of the spiritual ideal becomes matter of experience.

In the following chapters I shall attempt to illustrate what has been here sketched.[5]

---

[5] Spinoza, thinking mathematically, declares that **omnis determinatio est negaiio;** a thing is determined or defined by limitation, that is by exclusion. Thinking spiritually, we shall say the exact opposite: *omnis determinatio est affirmatio.* It is true in a sense that a man is a man in so far as he is not a woman, in so far as he excludes the qualities of the opposite sex; but spiritually it is true that a man becomes a man, in marriage for instance, in so far as he seeks to elicit the best in woman, the essential womanliness of her and thereby himself modified. It is true that the parent is not a child, but he becomes a true parent in so far as he seeks to elicit the best that is in the child, the essential nature of the child, and is thereby modified. And so throughout the groups and all the relations. We have here a conception of personality that distinguishes it from individuality. The individual is the subject that is to be personalized. The individual becomes a personality in and through his relations as he passes from group to group, from the less complex into the more complex, and thus approaches, at however great a distance, the infinite society, with its infinite scheme of interconnectedness. But the ideal spiritual society, or the rule derived from it, must guide his progress within each group, and as he passes from group to group at every stage

III

MARRIAGE

A YOUNG married: woman of my acquaintance recently astonished her friends by announcing her intention to divorce her husband. Was she unhappy? Had she reason to complain of him? Not in the least. On the contrary, she was fondly, devotedly attached to him, as he to her. It was her intention, to go on living with him as before. Why, then, the divorce? Because she simply could not bear the idea of a binding tie, of any relation which, pleasing though it might be, had- in it an element of compulsion. The mental attitude of this amiable young wife is profoundly symptomatic. Not the tie, but the presumption of permanence, the pledging of the will beyond the present moment is repugnant to her. And the widespread revolt against what is called in general bourgeois morality, and against the marriage institution in particular, is to no small extent attributable to the same cause, namely, impatience of constraint in any form, a certain emotional thin-skin-nedness that chafes under binding ties, finds them intolerable, and seeks to shake them off. And because marriage is that relation in which the binding tie is most intimate, and where nature itself seems to impose constraint in the fact of offspring, the attack on marriage is more vehement and convulsive than on any other of the social institutions, and marriage has become the storm centre of the modern revolt.

Georg Brandes, the Scandinavian critic, a literary authority of the first rank, exhibits much the same mental attitude. Speaking of Bjornson in a letter to Nietzsche, he declares that he is maddened to think that Bjornson should still hold to the belief in the marriage institution. It is true he concedes that for the multitude there is as yet no substitute; but that the elect, the enlightened, should still accept the tradition of monogamy maddens him. "Maddens" seems a curious word. If he had said astonishes, or even revolts, one could, from his point of view, understand; but the kind of exasperation—the being beside oneself expressed by "maddens"—reveals the psychic thin-skinnedness of which I have just spoken.

We are concerned here with the ideal of marriage, not simply or principally with the facts of marriage as they appear on a survey of modern society in civilised countries. An ideal is the mental image of a thing desired, not yet realised, or only in part realised. The ideal of the relation between the sexes is such an image of that relation as the contemplating mind would rest satisfied with. Now different minds will take different views of what constitutes a satisfactory relation. Some may define it as one which conduces to the happiness of the individuals in question, others as a relation which makes for the good of society; others, again, may try to combine the two points of view; but whatever the image which wins mental assent, it would be manifestly unfair to judge the ideal

out of hand and absolutely by the degree to
which it is carried out in practice. The ideal is
indeed a factor, and a most important one, in
influencing men's conduct. There are *idees-*
forces, to borrow Fouillee's phrase, and their
potency in human affairs cannot be denied. But
these *idees-forces* must enter into combination
with other forces such as peremptory appetites,
explosive passions, fantastic imaginings,
ruthless egotisms; and in the final result it is far
from easy, nay impossible, to assign to the
several components their share in producing the
result. The ideal is the form; human nature, with
its excesses and defects, is the matter. The
form should penetrate the matter, but it's
worth cannot be estimated by the degree
with which it has succeeded in doing so at
any one time, or at any one stage in the development of the human species. The worth of
an ideal is determined by two criteria:
does it, when beheld in its purity, commend
itself to the mind; and does it on the whole
tend, is it in its nature to bring into progressive conformity to itself the practice of men?

The subject I have undertaken to discuss is whether permanence or impermanence in marriage represents the true ideal, but, before entering on the argument, I should like to submit certain considerations which may help us to reach a just conclusion.

1. Marriage as the foundation of the family is one of the social institutions. It is important for my purpose to distinguish between social and ethical, to point out that a social institution is not as such an ethical institution. It may be a very unethical institution. In tracing the meaning of the word social, we find, to begin with, that it connotes the opposite of solitary. A solitary burglar, for instance, would be one who plays a lone hand in a criminal enterprise; a social burglar would be the member 6f a band engaged on similar business. Social in its primary use means simply "associated" with regard to some purpose, whether commendable or nefarious. Then, by an easy transition, it comes to denote, not bare association, but interdependence. A social re-

lation in this sense arises when several persons are mutually dependent, on the principle of *Do ut des*—I satisfy a certain want of yours on condition that you satisfy a certain want of mine. If human beings were self-sufficing there would be no occasion for the subdivision of functions, and consequently no social relations. The self-sufficing God of Aristotle is an eternally solitary being. Nevertheless, though men are compelled to exchange services, to interlock, as it were, it does not follow that the terms on which the exchange is effected need be or are just. A relation strictly social may be most unjust—for example, that of the master and the slave. Here the test of sociality is undoubtedly met, there is interdependence, there is exchange of services. The master gives food and shelter, the slave gives his labor and liberty. The relation is social, but certainly not ethical. Or take the relation of the Roman father, armed with the *patria potestas,* to the son, or the relation of the British mill owners to their so-called "hands," during the early decades of the last century—not to introduce examples from nearer home. And in like manner there exists a social relation in marriage and a social institution founded on that relation where the exchange of services' is at the basest level (cf. Immanuel Kant's amazing definition of the marriage compact), or where, on a higher level, the supremacy of the man over the woman is asserted without the slightest opposition on her side, and with the approval of public opinion. But the ethical relation, in contradistinction to the social, is that in which the supreme interest of each individual is achieved in complete harmony with that of all the others. And let us be clear upon the point that such har-mony has never yet been realised, that it is an ideal. No social relation has ever become a completely ethical relation, no social in stitution is worthy of being' dignified as an entirely ethical institution. A distinguished churchman says that there has never been a decent government on this earth—of course

not, if by decent we are to understand a
political organisation in which the genuine
interests of all the groups that compose the
State, and of the individuals that compose
the groups, are conciliated, or, one may add,
in which there is even the determinate
purpose on the part of the government to
harmonise them. And so we have no
difficulty in conceding to the assailants of
marriage that this particular social
institution, like the rest, has never yet
conformed to the ethical norm, if they will
allow that there is a norm. There are no
doubt degrees of approximation, and in the
absence of absolute perfection we shall not
simply confound the higher with the lower.
But even in the most nearly harmonious
marriages there is still an inextinguishable
residuum of defect. The ethical relation of
the sexes is a problem, not a datum, and the
best marriages are those in which the sense
of the problem as yet to be solved is vivid,
and the attempt to transform the actual after

the image of the ideal is unrelaxed.[1]

2. Human relations are to a very large extent chance relations, and in particular it is a matter of chance whether persons to whom we are bound by indissoluble ties are congenial or uncongenial. A child cannot divorce its parents, cannot cancel the fact that it is their offspring—a fact which carries with it certain prime obligations. And yet it is notorious that fathers and mothers on one side, and sons and daughters on the other, are often naturally antipathetic. Indeed, one's own child may in a certain sense

---

[1] have pointed out'above the difference between the two terms Social and Ethical. It seems to me unfortunate that this difference is so often overlooked. It is an instance of the slippery use of the moral vocabulary due to the lack of explicit analysis, and sure to breed confusion in practice. People speak eulogistically of the social attitude of mind, of the social spirit, arid the like, as if the social point of view were necessarily and of itself a commendable one. As a rule, they intend thereby to oppose the selfishly individualistic point of view—that is to say, they pass from one horn of the dilemma to the opposite. The Individual *v.* Society is the case in court. Shall society he sacrificed[1] to the individual, shall egotism dominate? No. Shall the individual be sacrificed to society, shall the State like a huge monster crush the man, shall the multitude submerge the individual? No, a thousand times no; But how shall ..the two factors be mediated? That is precisely the ethical problem. To emphasise the word Social as if it were synonymous with Ethical is to obscure the problem, to insist on one element, whereas the problem is to bring about an agreement of the two.

not be one's own child at all, may by some trick of heredity reproduce the features and character traits of some relative whom we detest. It is an accident whether we belong to one nation or to another, whether we happen to be Englishmen, Frenchmen, Americans. It is a matter of chance whether we were brought up as Mohammedans, as Buddhists, as Jews, or as Christians. A distinguished statesman once said to me: "Has not your reading of history taught you that chance rules the affairs of men?" I should not be willing to subscribe to this statement without qualification, but certainly the role of chance in human affairs is commonly underrated. And above all, chance is the supreme matchmaker, joining together as – often as not the uncongenial. Strictly speaking, it would be correct to say *always* joining together those who in some measure are unfitted for one another. For in no human pair is the man ever absolutely the counterpart of the woman and she of him. For as no two faces are alike, so no two characters are alike. There are ever irreducible idiosyncrasies, and it were indeed a miracle if the idiosyncrasies on one side were exactly suited to make a harmonious chord with the idiosyncrasies on the other. There are always at least latent discords, we do not naturally fall into tune with one another. The Platonic fancy of the two halves of the soul uniting is a myth. It is enough for "human nature's daily need" that there be some powerful initial attraction, some genuine fund of congeniality to be augmented and perfected as time goes on. Perfect congeniality is to be created, not found; to be approximated to, not to be presumed.

The ethical rule applied to human relations is to treat chance relations as if they were necessary relations, to transform them into necessary relations; to treat a companion whom chance has associated with us as if he were indispensable to us in the attainment of our supreme end. But the full meaning of this will appear later on.

In this connection a disconcerting counter-influence is to be noted, a trick of what the Hindus called the great Maya, that tendency to illusion which plays such havoc in the affairs of men. The illusion is that the perfect ideal of the relation of the man and the woman can be realised in marriage, that nothing short of entire fulfillment is to be expected, is to be insisted on. Any passionate attachment between persons of opposite sex is apt to be accompanied by this illusion. The object of the passion, the infatuation, is invested with the robe of perfection, worship passes into idolatry. Sometimes the idolatry is kept up obstinately, vitiating the relation by an intrinsic untruth—more frequently disenchantment follows. In no other human relation is this trick of illusion so strong. No one expects as a citizen to live in the perfect state; no one engaged in a vocation, however lofty, expects to see the highest ideal of that vocation realised, either in himself or in his colleagues. In marriage it seems otherwise.

And among the causes that lead to the unrest, and the bitter complaints about the failure of marriage, is its failure to fulfil the seductive dream that haunts the minds of those who are uninstructed as to the relation of the ideal to the actual.

3. In marriage and the family two instincts are operative—the sex instinct and the parental instinct. The two are often at cross purposes. The sex instinct in its raw state tends toward the impermanence of the relation, the parental relation tends toward permanence. The sex instinct in its raw state (without those sublimations superinduced by aesthetic and moral cultivation), is unstable, capricious, inappeasable, restlessly transitive, the substance of insubstantiality, compact of infidelity and change. The parental instinct, on the contrary, knits together the man and the woman in their offspring, indirectly but so firmly as to make their separation in any case painful. At present the parental instinct seems to have been weakened in many instances, partly

owing to the migratory habits of the population, the children quitting the home at an early age to shift for themselves, partly owing to the erroneous opinion encouraged by Socialism that systematic education by scientific teachers in public institutions is preferable to unsystematic bringing up by parents who yet, whatever else they lack, do supply the indispensable element of unique personal interest and cherishing affection. At any rate the fact that in so many recent writings on the subject the ideal of marriage is depicted as if it were a relation solely between the man and the woman (a sex relation), minimising the existence of children, treating their existence almost as negligible, indicates that in the minds of these writers and their following one of the two instincts, the sex instinct, predominates over the other. Yet one cannot help thinking that this state of feeling, after all, must be exceptional and temporary, for in any large survey of the past one perceives that in human beings the parental instinct predominates.

All that is best in human civilisation has been built up on the basis of the long infancy of children, and the character traits developed^ in parents by the direct personal dependence upon them of their children, and it seems likely that in the future, as in the past, this ingrained tendency will hold its own. One reason why we should desire that it will is that the sex relation itself is chiefly dignified by its orientation toward the parental.

4. The doctrine that the happiness of the pair is the sole or the principal object of marriage is a novel one. Happiness is a thing naturally and universally desired, but it is not therefore set up as the chief desideratum, except at a time when the subjective aspect of life eclipses the objective—that is to say, when the individual conceives of himself in an abstract way as having rights apart from his social connections, and estimates his gelations to others, and even the services he cannot help rendering- them, according to the degree of pleasure which he derives from

such relations arid services. Marriage plainly has an objective side as well as a subjective, and the former must predominate Over the latter. As much happiness as is achievable—yes, but not happiness the paramount end. Indeed, the most real happiness, the utmost peace and satisfaction, is to be attained only by identifying the objective with the subjective purpose. Ask not and ye shall receive. Emerson somewhere has it that the beauty of a sunrise or a sunset is most entrancing when it comes as a surprise by the way, not when deliberately sought. It is the same with happiness. .The obvious purpose of marriage is to perpetuate human life on earth, and not only human life but human civilisation—-that is, the life of human beings as ordered on a certain plan, with a view to maintaining certain public human interests deemed essential. . To these public interests the private interests of the married pair have ever in the main yielded preference.

As to what are the genuine public interests, however, there have been curious misjudgments due to the imperfect stage of social development reached, and entailing often great and cruel hardship. The marriage alliances of royal houses are an example. The so-called "reason of state" prevailing, the public interest was identified with the territorial aggrandisement of the ruling dynasty. The intimate preferences and aversions of the princely personages were disregarded, the man or the woman was sacrificed to the fetish of political power. Under the feudal *regime* landed property was the fetish. Human beings were regarded in a way as adjuncts to the estate; the transmission of the estate unimpaired, and if possible enlarged, was regarded as the public interest to be perpetuated by marriage. In the artisan corporations, broadly speaking, the object of marriage was to recruit the guild—the son stepping into the shoes of the father, and the public interest was conceived as maintenance of the vocational *status quo.* Society in general at that time was unprogressive; civilisation, at least in theory, was immobile, and was to be kept so; the social order such as it existed was to be maintained, and marriage was the instrument for thus maintaining it.

The dynastic, the feudal, the guild conceptions of the public interest have now disappeared. The family is no longer regarded as the organ designated to fill the ranks of a stable society'—it is the vestibule that leads into a great variety of vocations. The son is not any longer expected to follow in the footsteps of his parent. The supposedly paramount ends of property and the like are no longer acknowledged as paramount. Individualism, on that side of it on which it represents" the inviolable personality of the man or the woman, righteously rebelled against human interests being subordinated to property interests. Property is a means to an end, the end being the development of personality, and to sacrifice the end to the means is preposterous. But the individual is only one of the factors to be considered in the ethical relation, the other is the group with its interests. And individualism to-day raises its head and towers into the clouds, because the group ends which have been proposed no longer command respect—neither the political organisation nor the social order as it exists, nor yet the institution of marriage, as its meaning is understood. And in default of an objective purpose deserving of veneration, it is natural that the subjective aspect should be uppermost, and that the happiness claim should be exaggerated.

This, to my way of thinking, accounts for the state of things to which we have come; and the state of things to which we have come is, for the proximate future at least, far from reassuring. It is not only the rapid progress of the divorce movement in all countries that indicates the spread of subjectivism, it is the fact that many admirable people, fine women among the rest, who themselves conform to established usages, nevertheless entertain and do not hesitate to express the opinion that impermanence in marriage would be the ideal arrangement. It is this fact, I say, that reveals the extent to which the foundations have been shaken. And let us frankly confess that it is not possible successfully to oppose the public interest to the private, to demand of self-respecting human beings that the one should simply give way to the other, that the public interest, like some monstrous steamroller, should be allowed to suppress the rightful claims of the private soul. Unless a way can be found of identifying the two, of planting, as it were, the public interest in the very heart of the private, of convincingly showing that it is the supreme interest of the private man or woman to be creative of the public interest, no solution will be in sight. Such a solution is possible only on the spiritual plane, and of this I shall presently have to speak. But before offering my own suggestions, I must advert briefly to the sacramental theory of marriage, which at the present day is the only one that holds the field, at least for those who remain under the influence of the Church, as against the widespread inundation of subjectively individualistic ideas and practices.

The sacramental theory undertakes to give a ground for the permanence of the marriage tie. Does it succeed in doing so? According to the theory, God is a third partner in every marriage solemnised by the priest. God unites the pair, and what God has joined liian may not put asunder. But what good reason is there for supposing that God did join together any particular pair, more particularly when the event proves that they were egregiously unfitted, maladjusted, or, as the phrase is, incompatible with one another. Does God link incompatibles together? Should he not be conceived as the author of harmony? Yes, if a single married pair existed harmonious in an absolute sense one might admit that the Deity had united them, adding that this particular pair may never be divorced—a superfluous addition, however, since, being absolutely harmonious, they could not and would not separate.

But the Church does presuppose the existence of incompatibilities, uncongenialities, and the real ground on which the Church of Rome, at all events, vindicates the indissoluble union is its belief in the miraculous efficacy of the sacrament. The sacrament is the cement, as it were, which holds together what would otherwise split off. St. Augustine declares that the sacrament alone, as administered by the priest, renders the recipients capable of living together permanently in conjugal fidelity. Conjugal fidelity, he says, is regarded as a noble ideal even by civilised peoples outside the Church, but without the magical sacramental touch human nature is incapable of living up to such an ideal. To the objection that adultery is known to occur after marriages celebrated by the priest, Augustine replies that the grace communicated in the sacrament remains indelible, but that it operates in the case of adultery so as to make the rebellion of the adulterer against grace a more heinous sin, just as in baptism it makes a crime committed after baptism a more hideous crime.

In Ephesians v, we have a more spiritual interpretation of marriage, and a more spiritual reason given why it should be permanent, namely, because the husband has a certain work to perform on behalf of his wife, which is never complete during their finite existence together. The relation between the woman and the man is depicted as analogous to that between the Church and Christ. As Christ is the head of the Church, so man is the head of the woman. The Church is the body of Christ, his earthly members. The analogy implies that the wife is to be regarded as the more earthly part in the union, it implies the supremacy of the man in marriage. Again, the phrase that Christ is the head of the Church implies that a certain influence proceeds from him and penetrates the Church. This influence, as the context shows, is that of overcoming the sense nature of the members of the

Church, of making the Church pure in the
sense of otherworldly. It follows again,
per viam analogies, that the work to be done
by the man on behalf of the woman, the
spiritual benefit he is to confer on her, is that
of overcoming the more passionate tendencies of her nature, of fixing in her mind the
otherworldly outlook. But this theory of
marriage involves identifying spirituality
with otherworldliness, it implies that the
woman is the more passionate of the two, a
contention which it would be difficult to sub-
stantiate, an echo of the Genesis story where
woman plays the part Of the temptress, and
it represents the spiritual relation as uni-
lateral, the man exercising the elevating influence, the woman being merely the recipi-
ent of it, while in truth reciprocality of
influence is of the very essence of the spiritual relation. The sacramental theory may still
be a bulwark of permanent marriage for the
members of the more orthodox churches,
but it will hardly serve the purpose for those
who have been taught to reflect upon the as-

sumptions of the theory. Nor will the bare
fiat expressed in the dictum "What God hath
joined let no man put asunder" suffice to im-
press those who, when required to subordinate their happiness to something higher,
expect to be furnished with an adequate
reason for so doing.[2]

Let us pause for a moment to consider the
point which we have reached. The perma-
nency of marriage is still intrenched in the
laws and usages of society, and deeper down in
the parental instinct; but habits may be
unlearned, and even strong instincts may become uncertain, unless supported by intellectual conviction, and a theory of marriage
justifying the permanence of the relation at
present is nowhere in sight. The authority
of the Church as far as it extends is useful as

---

[2] Perhaps it might be argued that an adequate reason is not
far to seek, seeing that the desire for happiness in impermanent
relations is self-defeating. Impermanence itself is one of the
chief causes of unhappiness, and, moreover, no one has ever
been able to describe a state of society which would be pleasing or even tolerable if temporary relations were to become
the rule. But this would mean to discredit impermanence without furnishing a reason for permanence—the conclusion might
then be that neither plan is acceptable, and that there is nothing
for it but a choice of evils.

a dyke against the flood. It is a restraining but not a constructive influence. While if we turn to the philosophers, especially the philosophical systems of recent times, we shall get but scant help from their teachings. What has Bergson to say that is helpful in solving the marriage problem, or Bertrand Russell, or the experimentalists? As for the great German philosophers, the two who are reputed the most ethical, Kant and Fichte, are quite impossible as guides. Kant's views on marriage are pitched on the lowest scale; Fichte's are curiously, ineptly romantic. Hegel's opinions on the social institutions are conservative, but one must swallow intellectual absolutism in order to be content with his reasons.

To know what we lack is the *sine qua non* of progress. There is no ethical theory of marriage in existence at present that serves. This must be set down plainly, decisively. with full knowledge of what is implied in the statement. By an ethical theory I understand one that shall respect and even heighten the claims of the individual, while at the same time proposing a supereminent end to which the private happiness may and should be subordinated.

The issue lies between the ideals of permanence and impermanence. We are bound to – decide which of these two ideals we sanction. Permanence becomes peremptory if a truly objective end can be proposed which the individual will recognise as superior to his private ends, which he will embrace as being indeed his own dearest end, in the pursuit of which his existence becomes worth while in his own eyes. An objective end is one that stands on its own feet. An objective end is like a beautiful work of art that has a value of its own independent of the subjective state of the individual who created it, of the pleasure he experiences or the pain he suffers in making it. It has a certain externality apart from its creator, and yet is intimately connected with him, for it expresses a trans-subjective value which he is capable of conceiving and to a certain extent embodying. No human action can be without a motive; the motive in this case is obedience to the impulsion from within, and the satisfaction is found in giving free course to the inner constraint, despite the distress or even the anguish by which it may be ac companied, and despite the incompleteness of the result. Or, to put it more positively, the objective end, and with it the permanence of marriage, will appeal in the long run to those in whom activity is predominant—they are, in my use of the word, the ethically-minded; while impermanence will be favoured by those in whom recipiency is predominant, who reflect in all their relations and all their exertions upon the quota of pleasure which they may derive therefrom.

To live in activity as such directed toward a worth-while object—the worth-whileness of the object radiating into the activity, even when the object is not attained—is one state of mind; to treasure the pleasantness of one's own feelings is a different state of mind.

Turning now to the arguments adduced by the advocates of impermanence, we find that we have to deal, firstly, with their con-

ception of freedom; secondly, with the meaning they attach to self-expression; and,
thirdly, with their dictum that where love
ceases marriage should cease. I referred in
the beginning to the young married woman
who sought a divorce because she could not
endure a binding tie, and to Brandes's exasperation as attributable to the same cause.
Freedom in these instances means the absence of binding ties, of constraint in any
-form. To indicate briefly my own standpoint, I will lay down that *binding ties are
welcome in so far as they are necessary to unbind what is highest in us.* Those binding
ties which do not serve this purpose, like
restrictions on the freedom of conscience, the
freedom of speech and the like, are censur-
able, and social progress largely consists in
undoing them. The other kind of binding ties are
to be affirmed, and social progress
largely consists in making them more binding, or one might say automatically effectual. Positive freedom is an expression of
the essential self in us; the question is

whether the tie, which permanently binds one man to one woman, is indispensable to freedom thus conceived. The issue is between wild freedom, neurotic freedom, and positive freedom.

Next, as to self-expression. I hope it will not seem too pedantic if I distinguish three aspects of the self,—not, of course, three selves, but three aspects of the self—the lower, the higher, and the highest, and predicate as corresponding to them the minor ends of a human being, the major ends, and the maximum end. As to the minor ends, the animal ends, those which, broadly speaking, we share with the inferior creatures, no one, I imagine, will deny that in case of collision they should give way to the higher ends. To advocate impermanence in the sex relation for the sake of a more varied gratification of the sex instinct would be to reduce man to the animal level, since in a life thus lived, a disorderly, dissipated life, the mind, being uneasily set on sense gratification, the higher faculties, those of the thinker, the artist, the mal of affairs, would stand no chance; the lower, groveling purposes would fill the horizon, the things that count from the human point of view would be out of the picture. Moreover, the general mental instability that goes with such an existence is unfavourable to that concentration which is so essential to any valid achievement in art or science or business. The unbinding of the animal instincts blocks The way to the exercise of the higher faculties. The binding of the lower is necessary in order that the higher may act. This, at least, is indisputably a condition of freedom, and it is proper that a certain coercion in this particular be exercised by society—that laws, for instance, against crime be enacted, laws which the more developed human beings voluntarily consent to and are never even tempted to infract, but which are useful and necessary to restrain the weaker brethren.

But the position for which I specially contend is that not only the lower should give way to the higher interests, but that the higher, the major ends, should give way to the highest, the maximum end, in case of collision; and this is the pivot on which, in the last analysis, the issue between imperma- nence and permanence turns. This is the point where the harmful ambiguity of what is called the right to self-expression has to be exposed.

The right of self-expression, as commonly understood, implies untrammeled oppor- tunity for the development of one's talents and tastes, of one's intellectual and aesthetic —that is, of one's higher—faculties, of those that subserve the major ends of life. But the major ends must yield precedence to the maximum end, the maximum end being the affirmation, not of the one or the other par- tial aspect of the self (the intellectual or aesthetic), but of the self as a whole, of the unique personality as postulated in others and in oneself. And this involves respect for the unique personality of others, and as a corollary the preservation of others so far as they depend on us for the sake of their unique personality. An instance in point is the action of a youth who was offered the chance of a university education, and who made what for him was the grand refusal, because his aged parents were dependent on him for support, and there was no one else to take his place. He sacrificed his intellectual ambitions, perfectly legitimate as they would have been in other circumstances. He sacrificed a major end for the sake of the maximum end, he sacrificed his higher self, so to speak, in order to express his highest self, and such self-expression has the character of sublimity.

The same applies to mothers in relation to their children. No one nowadays questions the right of a woman to follow any vocation to which she is inclined, and for which she believes herself fit. Astronomy, chemistry, among the sciences, law, music, literature, the banking business, are a few of the walks of life in which women have essayed their power. No one questions their right to go

as far as they possibly can. But neither for
women nor men is it possible to follow two
vocations at the same time. For every real
vocation is exigent, and is becoming more
and more so. It is desirable to have an avocation alongside of the vocation, but it is not
practicable to have two vocations, to serve
two masters. Goethe tried it and failed, and
he condensed his experience, toward the
latter part of his life, in the words: "Work
and renounce" *(Entsagen sollst du, sollst entsagen)*; work assiduously in thine own line,
and try to develop thy talents and tastes in
other directions only to the extent that is
consistent with the most efficient perform^
ance of thine own task. Now motherhood
is, or at least in the way of becoming, a true
vocation. It draws upon various sciences—
on chemistry, physiology, on psychology, on the
applied arts, on applied ethics, the theory
of punishment for instance—and besides,
since the family is the foundation of the
State, and the right ordering of the State
reacts upon the family, the wiser mother-

hood implies active participation in public life. The mother is no longer restricted, or supposed to be restricted, within the four walls of her house, but her interests and activities are nevertheless vocationally focalized upon the life problems of the members of the group which centres in her as the mother. The single woman may choose any profession she pleases, but a married woman has her profession cut out for her. She may continue to have her avocation alongside, her music for instance, but if she have children she can hardly expect to be a professional musician, unless indeed she is willing to delegate the care of her children to paid assistants. A married woman therefore may have to sacrifice the higher interests of intellectual and aesthetic development, to forego the development of certain talents and tastes in order to revere the maximum end, which is regard for the personality of those who depend on her. The question, here as elsewhere where self-expression is raised as an issue, is which of your selves do you desire to express, the higher or the highest?

But how do we stand toward the dictum that love alone consecrates the sex life? As against mercenary marriages, the *mariage de convenance,* marriage for wealth or title or the like, it is obviously valid. I have said above that absolute congeniality is a dream, but a certain fund of congeniality, a certain intimate attraction there ought to be to warrant the hope of augmenting and perfecting it later on. But before we agree to the inference that where love ceases marriage should cease, had we not better pause to inquire in what sense the word "love" is used. It cannot mean the passion of the libertine, for in that case why speak of marriage? Illicit relations are avowedly temporary. The understanding on either side is that there shall be no responsibility, and therefore no permanence. It is just the absence of responsibility that appeals to the lovers of the wild freedom. It cannot surely mean that marriage is to cease when the physical charms of the woman diminish, a change which often takes place after childbirth, just at the time when the fact of responsibility stands out most Unmistakably. If that were the meaning, then marriage would be a mere cloak for promiscuity. But the plea that marriage should cease when love ceases is put forward by finer natures, and in their case it is based on an aesthetic ideal of life.

Let me here introduce a word as to the difference between the aesthetic and the ethical point of view. The aesthetic temperament is distinguished from the ethical in that it seeks to enjoy perfection here and now, while the latter endeavours to create perfection, and is willing to suffer the pain of imperfection while engaged in the effort of creation. For as much as a person is what I have called ethical minded, it does not follow that he is insensitive to beauty, to the harmonies of sound, colour, line, etc., achieved by art. He will delight in them as recreations of the spirit, as stimulations for his proper task, as foreshadowings of those harmonies which the ethical ideal requires that he seek to actualise in human lives. The cesthetically-minded person feeds on the perfections of art, reposes on them as finalities, and when, leaving the domain of pure art, he faces the problem of associating with his fellow beings, who are not as ductile to the artistic touch as sounds and colours and lines, he refuses to take his share in the slow process of transforming human nature, and invents instead an illusory art of living on the plan of selecting for companionship those natures which are or seem to be already congruous with his own, and in whose society he hopes to enjoy even now the perfect harmony. Enjoyment of perfection on the one hand, working for the creation of perfection on the other, is the distinction.

As applied to the relation of men and women in marriage the aesthetic ideal maybe defined as the ideal of mutual complementation, deficiency on one side to be rounded out by quality on the other; insights, intuitions, delicacies on the one side to be compensated by stronger intellectual outreachings, volitional persistences, etc., on the other, the two natures thus falling naturally and increasingly into tune, and each experiencing the more complete expression of the individual self in consequence of the action upon it of the other self. Where, however, a mistake was made in the choice, where the partner fails to come up to expectations, where incompatibilities, at first unnoticed, appear after marriage—and it is precisely these incompatibilities that appear after marriage which constitute the real problem—then from the aesthetic point of view, and in the name of love, the marriage is to be dissolved, and the ideal partner sought elsewhere—a wild-goose chase if ever there was one.

From the ethical standpoint, the notion of mutual complementation as thus put forward must be strenuously combated. Just because it is so fine, so fascinating, and yet does not ring true, the falseness in it, the perils which it harbors, must be shown up. A certain objective end is to be pursued by the married partners greater and more worth while than the finest mutually egotistic satisfactions. My thesis is that even in the most fortunate marriages a residue of incompatibility remains; nay, I go so far as to say that as individuation proceeds, idiosyncrasies will develop more intimate and difficult to match. My thesis further is, that wherever there is friction the conflict of impulses and desires can only be overcome by pointing to some overarching supereminent end, some commancing purpose which the persons concerned alike recognise, effecting unity through cooperation in the effort to accomplish that purpose. This holds good in regard to the friction between the social groups, in regard to the conflicts of nations, in regard to the incompatibilities that appear in marriage. There must be some over-arching' end in view clearly discerned; the absence of such an end from the minds of men is the radical ethical weakness of our age. Cooperation, then, not complementation! Complementation, at least as the idea

is understood, is a compact for the exchange
of egotisms. I can best gratify my selfish
purpose by ministering to yours, and you in
turn by ministering to mine. The selfish
purpose in the case considered is the expression of the higher self, not of the highest.
When we look at the highest we find that
the satisfaction which it craves, no longer
subjective, consists, as has been said, in the
production of an independent good which
has indubitable significance in the nature of
things, aside from the pleasures and pains of
the beings that are engaged in producing it.
And cooperation in the effort which is subservient to that end is the keynote of conjugal love in its purest, most spiritual aspect.
We love the person who is most precious to
us in the sense of making our life most admirable, in securing self-respect on the
loftiest terms. As fathers or mothers there
is only one person in the world who is indispensable to us in this way, and this is the
woman or the man with whom we are associated in marriage; for as fathers and

mothers the attainment of our highest self-respect depends on our relation to the child, and as there is only one person associated with us in giving life to the child, there is no other upon whom we can count to render us this supreme service.

But let me define more exactly the over-arching end to which marriage is devoted, the task which the man and the woman are to fulfil jointly. Marriage is the organ for the perpetuation of the spiritual life, which, so far as we know, appears in the finite world only in human beings. The spiritual life is a feeble flame that needs to be continuously replenished. and the vehicles of it, men and women, how frail are they, and how brief is their hold on existence! The trees of the forest survive us, the rocks outlast us by millenniums. If it were not for reproduction, this human race of torchbearers would become extinct, and with it the flame of which it is the bearer. Every married pair undertakes to fulfil on its part the task of humanity. This is the obligation which all who enter into the marriage relation should have before their minds. But the task is not only to perpetuate the spiritual life, but to enhance it—that is, to extend the reign of spirit on earth, to heighten its quality, to produce in human relations an image of "the Kingdom of Heaven"--that is, to transfigure as far as may be the natural relations between human beings into spiritual relations. Now the spiritual relation itself is nothing else than an ideally organic relation, one in which the organic idea, whereof we have no adequate example whatever, either in the animal or the human world, is conceived as perfectly realised—that is to say, a relation of distinctively differentiated functions so interacting that each in its exercise promotes the absolutely efficient exercise of the rest, with which it is systematically co-related. The conclusion is that marriage is spiritualised when each of the two sexes so acts as to draw out the distinctive sex quality of the other in respect to mind and character, and in so doing achieves its own—that is to say, when the essential womanliness of the one elicits the essential manliness of the other, and conversely, each in so doing becoming possessed of its own essential and distinctive quality. The formula of the spiritual relation is: So act as to elicit the best in others, in the process eliciting the best that is potential in thyself.

As to what is this essential womanliness, this essential manliness, there may be different opinions. The psycho-physical nature with which we are endowed is the basis on which the spiritual is to be superinduced, and our knowledge of the psychology of sex is still in its infancy. But perhaps I may be permitted to suggest the following: The peculiar gift of woman, it seem to me, is to see life as a whole—hers is, as it were, the assembling function; the peculiar gift of man is specialisation, the exercise of energy along specific lines. The whole which the woman sees is not indeed the whole of life; it may be, and generally is, only a section of life, often a narrowly circumscribed section—her social set, a certain parochial environment, a church fellowship—but that which she sees she is apt to see together, as a whole. The influence of man should be to enlarge her world view more and more, to widen her horizon; and ideally the influence of woman upon man as he enters into the complexities of life, should be to help him to systematize the relations in which he finds himself, to order his purposes on a synoptic plan, to harmonize all his relations—to .herself, to the children, if there be children, to the members of his vocation, his fellow workers, to the State of which he is a citizen, to humanity, to the universe. Ideally, and I am here speaking of supreme ideals, the woman represents the total world spirit, she is "the Eternal Womanly that leads man upward and onward," she is the solar, centralising influence, she is the Woman clothed with the Sun, she is Beatrice standing on the heights of heaven surveying the infinite scheme of things, and with the smile which radiates the beauty of her being contenting man with his place.

Some measure of such influence the two sexes , may exert upon each other in their friendships, and more deeply in childless marriages; but it is the responsibility for the child, their common offspring, that most effectively calls out the interaction between them, inciting them to win the greatest possible spiritual profit out of their intercourse with one another—in order that on their part they may fulfil the task of mankind, which is to enhance the spiritual life of the next generation by planting the seed of spirit in their own child which, so far as they are concerned, stands for future humanity. The child is the seal of the marriage compact. The responsibility to the child is the incentive that should incessantly draw out all that is best in either, in order that they may transmit that best for prospective increase to their successors in life.

Those who believe that a theory of marriage can be constructed without reference to the child ignore the peculiar good which it is the prerogative of parents to bestow

upon children, and the peculiar ethical reaction which they get in return. A word as
to this. In all our dealings with our fellowmen the ethical view requires that we attribute to them a certain potential worth-
whileness, apart from any actual value which
they may have, and even in despite of their
being actually nuisances and impediments to
progress. The ethical view requires us to
consider no fellow man as hopeless. It insists always on the potential in defiance of
the actual. It is this that forbids us to ex-
terminate even degenerates or hardened
criminals; it is this that led Jesus to find dis-
ciples among harlots and tools of the Roman
system of extortion (the publicans). Humanity has worth apart from value, worth
being the potential quality. Now parents—
the mother especially, but the father also
more indirectly—instinctively hold the child
unspeakably worth while, in advance of any
value which it could possibly claim, in advance of any deserving on its part. To the
child this being held so precious at the out-

set of life gives a sense of security, a sense of being at home somewhere in the world. It affords a kind of anchorage to which to attach its moral personality; while for those parents at least who transcend their instinctive impulses, the feeling they have for the child is a support for their ethical attitude toward human beings in general. Never can the goodwill of trained teachers in a public institution, or the fraternity feeling upon which Socialism relies, take the place of this preferential relation of parents and children and the ethical, experience into which it may be developed.

Concentration, I remarked above, is indispensable to the thorough performance of any great task—in science, in the arts, in affairs; it is certainly no less indispensable in the sublime task of searching out the essential personality of a woman, the essential personality of a man, of penetrating to the roots of the other's self, of gripping the uniqueness that so hides itself, though it is .there, at least the idea of it—of bringing it to the surface, of making it an effectual *idee force.* Concentration, therefore, on one woman or on one man, in other words permanence in the marriage relation, is the spiritual *sine qua non.* This searching for the hidden, divine thing by each in the other, with the assurance that though elusive it exists, this yearning toward it, this foreknowledge that the complete union between the two souls can only be achieved at the summit of the nature of each—this, to my mind, is love, as it is known at its truest. And because the search, in the nature of the case, is perpetual, therefore the union must be perpetual. And we may say to those who insist that when love ceases marriage should cease: You are right, friends, only that what you say is a truism, for it is in the na-ture of the thing that properly appropriates the world love that it shall never cease. The circumstances that it cannot cease is the very test and touchstone by which it may be distinguished from its fair or foul semblances.

I have set out in this book to apply a certain spiritual ideal to the vital problems of modern life, of which marriage is one. But I shall now be told that I have traveled too far away from the actual facts, and that the ideal is too airy to be applicable. Take the case, for instance, of a superior man who finds himself tied for life to a frivolous woman, a woman of inferior mental capacity, who is dull to all the things that really interest him—can there be spiritual companionship between these two? And will not the man, supposing that he is courageous enough to disregard the restraints of convention, consider himself justified in putting an end to the relation? The case may easily be reversed, the woman being the superior, but to avoid circumlocution let me adhere to the first way of putting it. Or even suppose that the two parties start on a fairly equal level, but that the one develops more rapidly than the other, and outdistances the other. Referring to what was said above as to the difference between the higher and the highest levels, my reply is that on the higher level, companionship may not be possible, but that on the highest, the spiritual level, it is. For spiritual companionship is a relation of personalities as a whole, and in the sex relation it is not just the intellect of the man that is to be mated with the intellect of the woman, but the integral man to the integral woman. And while this relation does require the *development* of personality on either side (the manifestation of worth in terms of value), nevertheless it implies fundamentally, and before all and above all, respect for personality, and the discarding of either by the other is contrary to such respect.

Moreover, the superior man, of whom we are speaking, if he go into the matter searchingly enough, may have a remarkable experience. He may, for example, find the tables turned against himself, he may be startled into inquiring as he never did before into the motives with which he married this woman. Was it because she was good-looking, or had certain pleasing ways, or in the expectation of comfort and caresses, or

because it flattered his vanity to see her pre-
side over the hospitalities of his house? He
may be asking whether he himself ever had
any really spiritual ideal of marriage, any
just conception of the office which a wife
might fulfil for her husband, and whether
he on his part had ever attempted to render
the correlative office, and if not, whether it
was to be wondered at that the relation
should become mean or unbearably common-
place. And then I imagine that our friend
the superior man may make a somewhat
humbler estimate of his superiority, may see
a vision of the possibilities of the marriage
relation such as had never dawned on him,
and this vision will undoubtedly change his
conduct, producing on his side a new attitude
toward the wife which possibly may meet
with a response. For not infrequently we
find that people with whom we habitually
associate show to strangers a certain fineness
in their nature which we never see, because
we have never called it out, because we have
been too precipitate in judging what may or

may not be expected of them. But if there be no response, the vision itself and the challenge of it, the spiritual growth which it induces, will be a compensation and consolation for what might otherwise have been sheer martyrdom.

The so-called conservative is one who advocates the *status quo* in regard to the marriage institution. I am not to be ranged on that side. I believe in conserving the good in those institutions which have been transmitted to us by our forbears, but believe also that the good can only be preserved by transforming it into the better. The good in marriage is the permanence of it, the unity of the two wills. But this unity of two has often been achieved by the suppression of one. Unity is indispensable for the advantage of all concerned, especially for the children, but it must come by consent, and that, as has been shown, can only be achieved by directing both wills toward an objective, Overarching end. The right of woman to the most complete mental development possible, which was refused in the past, must be insisted on, not only in the interests of woman but of society in general. The outrageous double standard, already rejected in theory, must give way in practice.

There are many other evils that need to be corrected; for instance, the hasty marriages of young people who drift or rush into a relation of whose responsibilities they have not the slightest conception. These should be prevented by law and education. The indictment framed against what Nordau petulantly called the "marriage lie," against bourgeois morality and the institution of marriage as a part of it, is also in many respects true. The comfortable mid-die class extol the family as the foundation of all the virtues, and yet they take no effective measures to abolish the slums in which the primary conditions of a decent family life are lacking. Bourgeois morality extols the chastity of woman, while the low pay of female wage-earners puts temptation in their way, not indeed irresistible temptation, as is sometimes extravagantly stated, yet often difficult to resist. Moreover, the cities reek with the social evil, and infidelities and brutalities in marriage are not infrequent, of which women are physically and morally the victims. Such evils as these are not to be extenuated by the defenders of marriage. They are in part the result of the present economic system, with which, however, the permanence of marriage is not bound up, in part the result of dark forces in human nature—appetites, ugly passions, streaks of primitive ferocity—with which every ideal has to contend. In any case, impermanence in marriage would not remedy these evils, but exacerbate them, and if it were adopted women in particular would be the greatest sufferers.

Also it should be said that there is another side to the picture. The increase of divorce is a grave symptom; but if the law were changed to permit the dissolution of marriage at will it is probable that the greater number of married couples would refuse to avail themselves of it—the parental instinct may be relied on to that extent. And again if there be no absolutely perfect marriages, there are many in which a degree of ethical development as well as of happiness is attained that is to be met with in no other human relationship. The common life ingenders common sympathy. A man must be very near, the level of the brute who does not feel a certain awe, and gratitude mingled with humility, toward the woman who, in a kind of crucifixion, gives birth to their first child. The solidarity of husband and wife toward the outside world tends to unite them. Sorrow, as at the grave of a beloved child, grief, as over an unfilial son or daughter, draws the tie closer, and makes it sacred. And the common experiences tend to promote not only sympathy, but mutual understanding, the ability to enter into the state of mind of the other, to live in the life of the other. For the sorrow of a mother, for instance, in the case of an unfilial son or daughter, is unlike that of the father. The man may be more hurt in his pride, the woman wounded in a deeper, more elemental feeling. Add to this that close companionship has at least the ethical advantage of counterbalancing egocentrism. Single men and single women, when living an independent life, are apt to be more or less shut up in the circle of their own ends, their thoughts are more apt to revolve about the self. In marriage and the family the centre of gravity is more apt to be transferred from the self to the others, thereby counteracting extreme individualism, producing, it may be, only an enlarged selfishness, which, however, is likely under the influences just mentioned to turn into something better.

As to extreme cases, divorce is, and in view of the present state of public opinion must still be, the legal remedy; separation, but without remarriage, is the ethical counsel of perfection. But whatever the legislation on the subject of divorce may be, or whatever changes may be effected in it, the object should be to strengthen, not to weaken, the presumption of permanence. To admit incompatibility as a cause would be to multiply incompatibilities, to encourage the self-seeking man or woman to regard every difference as intolerable; while to grant divorce, as has happened recently, a second, third, or even a fifth time, is scandalous.

The outcome of the discussion may be summarised in the following statements:

I. The interests of the child—that is, the spiritual interests of future humanity—must be raised to prominence in the theory of marriage as against the prominence at present unduly accorded to the happiness of the man and the woman—the objective end must prevail over the subjective.

2. Binding ties are to be welcomed in so far as they unbind in man the higher and the highest.

3. Even the higher itself must be subordinated to the highest, the major ends to the maximum end in case of collision.

4. It is true that marriage should cease when love ceases. But it is in the nature of that love which deserves the name not to cease. We love that which is lovable. That which is most lovable is the secret beauty in another's nature. Love is the feeling evoked by anticipation of union with that beauty. It constantly recreates itself and is intensified even while thwarted. It is a longing anticipating its satisfaction; it is the constant unwillingness to be separated from the object of its quest.

IV

SOCIAL RECONSTRUCTION

T WO systems are mainly in view at present—capitalism on the one hand and socialism of various kinds on the other. We are here concerned, not with systems or schemes, but with principles. I shall therefore briefly consider the principles underlying[1] capitalism and socialism, and then call attention to a third principle, the organic or spiritual.[1]

A powerful motive underlies capitalism, that of individualistic self-satisfaction and self-affirmation as expressed in the phrase *la carriere ouverte aux talents*—with some-

---

[1] In popular debate the issue has unfortunately been narrowed down to this single pair of alternatives. Either one is a defender of capitalism or a socialist of some sort, one or the other. To criticise socialism is to publish oneself an advocate of the present competitive system. To censure that system is to be numbered with the socialists. That there is a third position possible, differing in principle from either, does not seem to have dawned upon' the public mind—I say differing in principle, and thereby^distinguished from opportunism or the *via media* method which' is guided by no principle whatever, but by what is rightly or wrongly, often wrongly, supposed to be practica. convenience.

thing like contempt for the less talented; or, again, the race to the strongest and swiftest, with but little heed to those who may be trodden under foot. And this motive is properly designated as materialistic, since the aim and object is the accumulation of material wealth, together with such social and political influence as the possession of riches secures. The so-called, harmony of interests, the argument that the unflinching egotism of each individual will somehow prove to be advantageous to all the rest, that the base metal in the economic crucible will somehow be transmuted into gold, is a mere afterthought—what would nowadays be called the rationalization of an unacknowledged craving, a craving so strong and nefarious that human nature shrinks from blankly confessing it. And a like rationalization is the argument that the prospect of unbounded wealth, first of thousands of dollars, then of millions, finally of multimillions, is the only magnet capable of drawing out the latent capabilities of inventors, ex-

ecutives, initiators of great enterprises; the
argument that unless the lion's share of
material goods falls to the few, the many
will not even have a modicum of such goods,
that Unless Dives feasts, Lazarus will not
even be able to pick up crumbs.

The economist may reprimand us at this
point for underestimating the merits of the
capitalistic system in the past, its historical
significance as the; successor of the feudal
organization of society, the value which may
still belong to it,, and the practical difficulty of replacing it. All this is very pertinent from the economist's point of view,
but it does not in the least touch the question with which we, looking to the future,
are here dealing: whether the motive that
keeps the capitalistic system going is honorable to men or not, whether it is the kind
of motive which, stripped of its rationaliza-
tions, can be satisfying even to those who
are prompted by it. We may indeed be told by
way of reply that human nature being
such as it is, no better motive could be found

to work. That may be so, or may not be so. At any rate it is a prejudgment, a belief founded on the way men behave under the existing system, which itself discourages better motives where they exist, and cannot therefore be taken to exclude the possibility that, given the proper kind of education, a more creditable system may become feasible.

The motive underlying socialism is likewise individualistic. Socialism is universalized individualism, individualism carried to its extreme boundaries. It differs, however, from the preceding system in two vital particulars. The happy career is to be open, not only to the talented, but to the untalented, the unskilled or the little skilled. All individuals are to be the recipients of benefit, and consequently the independent efforts of the stronger and more gifted are to be restrained and regulated by collective action. Under the competitive system every one hunts on his own account; under socialism the whole mass works for each member of it.

In either scheme the individual is the object aimed at. In the one scheme some individuals, but not all, in the other scheme all individuals. In the one scheme the well-being of the individual depends solely on his own exertions, in the other scheme it is secured by combination and reglementation.

Again, in either scheme the individual is considered solely and simply as a product of nature, without regard to the spiritual part of him. Marxist socialism is hostile to religion; the other, the competitive system, is as such indifferent to religion, leaves religion out in the cold—at any rate, in the competitive system, there is not the slightest trace of the influence of spiritual ideas. Wealth is defined exclusively in terms of man's natural wants and their satisfaction, and the heavy emphasis in the debate between the two systems falls on the distribution of wealth, whether the few shall have a preferential lien on the products of human labor, or whether the product should as far as possible go in equal shares to all.

It seems to me that a similar motive works in the competitive system and in socialism, at least in "scientific socialism." Both are individualistic and naturalistic, though the latter is inclusive of all individuals.

But does not the greatest possible dissimilarity appear in the exclusiveness on the one side and the inclusiveness on the other side? To say that all men are to have an equal share, does not that imply a profound moral impulse? And a moral impulse implies the conscious or unconscious acknowledgment of man as having spiritual needs, as well as natural wants, above all as having a personality not to be violated. Among many who call themselves socialists, no doubt the moral impulse is the decisive one, but "scientific socialism" ridicules their idealogies, allows for no excursions beyond the domain of the palpable. And it is scientific socialism that more than any other kind has captured the working classes; and of all the different variants of socialism it is still by far the most influential. On what ground then does it rest the claim that all individuals should be included? Obviously on the ground that they want to be, that they want material satisfactions; or, if they are servile enough not effectively to want them, that they can be stirred up to want them. To talk of rights is pure ideology. "Right" is a moral term. Rights as such do not count—force counts. The large masses of workers collected in modern industrial plants possess force. Let them be taught to use it. Hence the importance attached to the class war, force on the one side being pitted against force on the other. On the one side Nietzsche will raise the cry: Whip the dogs back to their kennels; on the other side the cry is Expropriate the expropriators!

The method of distributing the product is the outstanding issue in the struggle of the social classes as waged to-day, though of course the augmentation of the product is also considered as being necessary to such distribution as will furnish material satisfaction for all. What the man will do with the wealth allotted to him is to be left pretty

much to his own predilections. The satisfactions desired are of course not merely animal.
I have said 'natural' I have not said 'animal'
wants. Among the natural wants are also
the satisfaction of intellectual curiosity and
the desire for the pleasures of taste. The
spiritual needs are different. These are left
out of account in the schemes of social reconstruction. On them we shall presently con-
centrate our attention.

In the dictum that all individuals shall
be included we agree with the socialists. In
the position that the spiritual need of all
individuals shall be placed in the foreground
we differ from them. The spiritual need involves for one thing that any proposed plan
of social betterment shall be judged in the
first instance by the effect it is likely to have
on the producer himself, not by its effect in
the better distribution of the product. The
producer is our main concern, the improvement of human nature, the evolution of man
toward a nobler type, not the multiplication of his creature comforts and enjoy-

ments. If the equitable distribution of the product be indispensable to the improvement of the producer, as it is, then it will come as a means to an end; but then the multiplication of the product will not be itself exalted as the end.[2]

---

[2] I am here dealing with what may be called the fallacy of provisionalism. Children are perishing by the thousands, it is said, owing to malnutrition. The labor of young, immature persons is being ruthlessly exploited. The housing conditions in the slums are appalling. Men willing to work are walking the streets in consequence of the reckless action of unenlightened or unscrupulous employers. Let us then apply ourselves with might and main to the correction of these palpable, incontestable evils, and work for the higher ideals of society later on. Now no doubt some headway can be made by working for these provisional ends. Sentiment, self-interest, can be appealed to, and the factors that make for unfairness can be made to yield to a certain extent, but only to a certain extent. Wages can be raised so long as their increase is consistent with the accumulation of profit. When, however, the cessation of profit itself is threatened, there is an end of concession. The motive, the principle that operates in the competitive system then stands forth as an insurmountable obstacle. Better housing can be supplied here and there by benevolent employers—a complete change in the housing system is resisted tooth and nail. Certain forms of the piratical instinct in business are prohibited; big business declares with self-complacency, we have seen a new light; but the same ruthless instinct, like a flood which is dyked at one point, breaks out in new quarters, under new modes or disguises.
There is no help for it. Man is actuated by motives, and unless the motives can be changed, there will be no steadfast, no large, last'fg improvement, even in material conditions. Unless a new respect for human nature as such can be won, the power will be lacking to support the efforts that are demanded, even toward material betterment. Unless the poorest of the poor are seen as beings having worth, the values to which they may justly lay claim will never be accorded to them. There will be a little lightening of their heavy burden, the scanty requirements of what is called a

The touchstone of any system of social betterment is whether it will better human beings, the betterment of conditions being a means to that end. But, it may be asked, does not socialism successfully pass this test? Do not its followers look forward to the reign of fraternity on earth? Do they not count on fraternity to make the opera-

---

"decent" way of living may be provided, so far as is compatible with the continued living in palaces of the rich; but social reconstruction in any thoroughgoing sense will not take place.

Moreover, by leading the masses into the class war, hatred is fostered inevitably, even though the war be directed'ostensibly against the system, and not against individuals; and by fixing attention on material wealth as the object to be gained by the working class, with the provisional exclusion of the higher gains, the mind of the masses will be more and more steeped in materialism, held fast in materialism.

² It is a notorious fact, however, that in no relation is friction more common, and more distressing, than between brothers. The first pair of brothers are an example. The tie of consanguinity is indeed favorable to mutual kindness between natures that happen t» be sympathetic. It is apt to strain to the breaking point the relation of those who are naturally antipathetic. They are thorns in each other's side. Ethically brotherhood must be considered as a means of creating respect and love by the unlike for the unlike. The word as at present used designates the sympathy of the like for the like.

² Plato, it is true, prescribes communism only for the members of the ruling class, in order *to* keep them united, and relies not so much on sympathy, as on common devotion to an intellectual and artistic ideal.

² The proverb says that one cannot touch pitch without being defiled; but modern chemistry has extracted from coal tar the most beautiful dyes, the most helpful medicaments.

²1 do not say industrial democracy, because that connotes

tion of their system possible? Yes, it will at once make socialism possible and be its flower and effulgence; and hence there will be, it is believed, a change in human beings themselves, a larger and sweeter motive will take the place of the egoistic.

Of the three catch phrases of the French Revolution, liberty is the favorite watchword of capitalism; fraternity and equality are appropriated by socialism—fraternity as a means of bringing about and maintaining equality, and, thereafter, as the psychical result of the equality attained. Men, having acquired the habit of looking on each other as equals, are expected to feel for each other as brothers.[4]

To put the matter briefly, the points implied in the above are three:

1. Fraternity will help to establish equality.

2. The fraternity feeling will maintain equality when established.

3. The fraternity feeling will be a new motive making human nature more excellent.

As to point one, fraternity is the sympathy felt by the like for the like. This does tend toward the establishment of equality. The working class to-day is militant. In the trenches, the distinctions of birth and even of rank tend to be more or less obliterated. Men are exposed to the same dangers, are moved by the same animosities and hopes of victory. There is brotherhood in arms. The same is true in the social war. The diversities of function and interest that actually subsist among the workers tend at least to be minimized.[5]

As to point two, assume that the battle is won, that the class of manual workers are in

---

[5] That they actually continue to operate, as between the craft unions and unskilled labor, is felt to be a great hindrance to the progress of the working class movement.

In the theory of socialism, the functional diversities of the workers are reduced to a common denominator. The brain-workers as well as the various manual workers are classed simply under the head of abstract work—the kind of work done being relatively ignored in comparison with the one fact that work is done. Never has abstraction been carried to a more extreme degree than by these empirical theorists who deride ideologies. The claim of a man to an equal share in the product is based on the fact that he renders his share of this abstract thing—work.

possession. They constitute the overwhelming majority. The brain workers will be their servants. Will the fraternity feeling continue to operate? Will it maintain equality after temporarily equality has been established? It is more than likely, it seems inevitable, that all the differences of interest, of function, will reappear, and that the system which in the main ignores these differences will not live.

Point three. This is the one that has the greatest significance for us, since we are concerned more for the improvement of the producer, than for the distribution of the product. Will the fraternity motive (understood as sympathy of the like for the like) ennoble mankind? The emphasis of Brotherhood at the present time is the sign of an honorable reaction against the unjust discriminations that have hitherto prevailed in the social system, against privilege founded on birth, against hierarchical authority founded on the pretension to supernatural gifts, against a hideous plutocracy. The emphasis on likeness is a rebound against the unfair, untenable distinctions that have been made between man and man. The real unlikenesses, however, subsist, are rooted in the nature of man, are not only ineffaceable, but the very condition and opportunity of the higher development of the race. Such are the diversities of sex, of talent, of national character and the like. The overstressing of fraternity, seen from this point of view, is a formidable menace to the moral progress of society, as appears, for instance, in the classical example of Plato's *Republic*. Fraternalism as the key relation abolishes the family, the closer relations between parents and children, between husbands and wives. It destroys those initial intimacies in which the strong ties between human beings are first formed, to be thereafter extended and multiplied. It cuts the roots of the trees in the hope that leaning on each other for support the forest will become a more compact whole. Every adult male is to be revered as a father, every adult woman as a mother; every youth is to be loved as a

brother, every maiden as a sister. It fails
to see that under the arrangements contemplated there will not be many fathers, but
no fathers, not many brothers and sisters,
but no brothers and sisters. It fails to
see that the closer relations are the soil
in which those reverences and loves spring
up that become enriched in the wider relations. A vague sympathy for all is to take
the place of the firm affection for the few.
But a house erected on sand cannot stand.

If, then, its effect in improving the human
being as such is the test of any system of
social reconstruction, socialism, as tried by
this test, cannot be approved. If fraternity
as described is to be the outcome of it, its
effect will be to dissipate the better feelings
and eventually not to ennoble, but to de-
grade, the human species.[8]

Having thus briefly considered capitalism and
socialism, and having insisted that they
must be tried and judged by their effect on
the producers, it is time to ask more definitely what kind of effect on the producer we

are demanding, what we mean by making human beings more excellent, by improving human nature. From the spiritual point of view the answer is explicit. The spiritual principle to be substituted for the individualistic or collectivistic principles is clear. As a spiritual being, man's commerce with the finite world has for its object to produce the consciousness of his infinite nature. He is not of course pure spirit; he is a psychophysical being as well, but he is to discharge even his animal functions in such a way as to testify to his spiritual character; more than that, he is to treat such functions as opportunities for the affirmation and confirmation of the loftier attributes. What, for instance, can be a more animal-like function than eating, supplying the bodily machine with fuel? And yet the human way of taking food is precisely that which places man at the greatest distance from the animal. The daily habit of the members of a household to sit down at a common table becomes the means of fostering the sense of family

Unity; the common repasts of literary and other societies are occasions for "The feast Of reason and the flow of soul;" the sacrificial banquets of the ancients were the rituals of religion however crude; the *agape* of the early Christians and the communion service down to the present illustrate how the touch of the spiritual upon the physical transforms the physical, makes a physical act instrumental to a spiritual meaning.

The same is true of the function of reproduction, which likewise assimilates man to the lower creatures, and yet more sublimely marks the difference between him and them; for the sex relation is not merely refined by love, but at its best it gives rise to the sense of an indissoluble connection of soul with soul. The god triumphs in the dust; the spiritual triumphs in subduing the physical to its own use. Not to walk through the world unspotted of the world, is the aim, holding up one's skirts as it were meticulously, so that they shall not be soiled; on the contrary, we are to take hold confidently of the things that seem most soiling, and to assoil them by the cleansing touch.[7]

The turn I am taking in the discussion of social reconstruction is to apply this same thought to physical work, to the work of a man's hands, as well as to every other kind of work. Eating has a physical object—to keep the body replenished; it has also another and higher purpose. The physical becomes the opportunity of asserting this higher purpose. Reproduction has a physical object—the preservation of the human species; alongside of this, superior to this, a spiritual purpose. The same idea, when applied, will in a sense transfigure the physical task of those who labor in the mills, by putting the function of the manual laborer in the same class with those other functions which serve physical ends, and at the same time lend themselves as subservient to the spiritual ends of man. This is the chief point

---

[7] The proverb says that one cannot touch pitch without being defiled; but modern chemistry has extracted from coal tar the most beautiful dyes, the most helpful medicaments.

I wish to bring out in the present chapter. What supremely matters is that this change of attitude be envisaged. On the problem of how it can be carried out in practice, I shall presently offer some reflections, but the changed point of view is what I have most at heart to urge.[8]

I shall next consider the idea of service, which in recent writings has been prominently put forward as offering the purer principle and the motive that is needed for social reconstruction. The performance of services by the members of society is unavoidable. The most hard-hided egotist, whatever his motives has got to render some service in order to get his gains. But where the intention is to perform service for the sake of private, selfish gain, it is almost

---

[8]   My readers will remember that I am' discussing principles and not schemes, still less panaceas. The physical needs are so imperative, and for the great majority of men still so meagrely satisfied that a change in the attitude toward work can only be expected to take place in the course of generations. Yet it matters momentously that the right goal be set up, and that the leaders of thought, in planning next steps, see to it ' that these steps be taken in the right direction.

certain to be ill performed. And above all, the man himself is likely to be debased by making service subordinate to income instead of income subordinate to service, thereby reversing the relation that morally should subsist between public and private ends.

The conception of service now commonly advocated puts the emphasis on the doing of things that are useful to the community, for the sake of the doing of them in the best possible way. The centre of gravity in a man's consciousness is to be transferred from his self to the multitude of his fellow beings. And it is believed that by such transference human nature will actually be improved, since each one will care more for the advantage of others than his own; and the test to which we insist on subjecting any and every plan of social reconstruction, it seems, might thus be met. Altruism, specialized in various kinds of social service, would be the solution.

In an industrial system arranged on such a plan there would be no more profits. The thirst for profits would be quenched. Neither would there be a struggle between the manual workers and the brain workers engaged in industry for the larger share of the product. The efficient performance of function would-be the prevailing motive. Pride in the performance of function would inspire the workers. There would, of course, be the necessary division of labor, the assignment of the different tasks to the different talents. There would be executives, managers, superintendents, hand workers. The scientists, engaged in the research laboratories that are now attached to great industrial plants would also, and perhaps preeminently, be reckoned among the functionaries of an industry; so would the artists, when connected with an industry.

But at this point it must be remembered that the different functions will tend, to breed different interests, diversity in the points of view. The scientist engaged in research is naturally interested in the outcome of his experiments; he is not as such interested in the manual laborers, to whom he prescribes the processes after he has discovered the formula. The executive, administrative officer is likely to be interested in creating a perfect machine, the foreman perhaps in getting the utmost quantity of work out of the workers. What, then, is to prevent friction? The answer of the service principle as described is: the bond of unity will be the common desire to benefit the community. But how to benefit them? By producing material goods such as serve for men's convenience and commodity; in the shoe industry, for instance, by producing shoes; in the textile industry by producing fabrics in the requisite quantity and quality. But will service, as expressed in such material satisfaction of mankind, disinfect the service of its materialistic taint? Will it truly ennoble the man who renders it?

In the previous chapter, when speaking of incompatibilities in marriage, of the clash between the sexes, I stated as a general rule to be observed in all relations where there is likely to be a conflict of interests and purposes, that such conflicts can only be overcome by presenting to the minds of the parties concerned an *overarching end,* an objective end loftier than their subjective ends, in the joint promotion of which they will express their real, essential selves. Is the production of shoes in the requisite quantity, and of fabrics in the requisite quantity, etc., an overarching end of this kind? Will it in the long run be found adequate to unify the factors that clash in industry?

Commerce with the finite, I have said in a previous paragraph, should be the means for man of asserting his infinite nature; work should be regarded like food taking and reproduction, as an occasion for the worker to achieve the consciousness of his spiritual relations. And this finally leads to the ideal organic principle of social reconstruction, as the one which is here submitted as fit to replace the individualistic competitive, the collectivist, and the specialized altruistic or the social service principle, as the latter is

commonly understood. In an industrial system planned on the ideally organic principle,
the personal relations will count above everything else, the development of the right personal relations between the unlike workers
will be the object aimed at. The making of
shoes is necessary, like the taking of food,
but the making of the shoes itself will come
to be regarded with a certain irony, as a
necessity to which spiritual beings in the
finite world are subject. It will not itself be
the *terminus ad quern* of their efforts, it will
be the means of creating between them certain personal relations, a certain ideally organic relation, namely a relation such that
each of the different functionaries will seek to
perform his task in such a way as to bring out
the best performance of their diverse tasks
by the others. I am dealing here with an
abstract principle; and every principle enunciated as a principle is abstract, but becomes
concrete in its application. Right personal
relations are human relations, and a human
being is never a mere hand; he has also

a mind and a will. The right personal relations would be for one thing the reciprocal stimulation of the intelligence of the workers. Every industry to-day is saturated with mind. Industry may be regarded as the pragmatic aspect of science, the executive application of science, and of invention based on science. The challenge coming from the side of industry has been a prime factor in bringing about the advances of science. The progress of the science of electricity is one example among a thousand. At present all that is high in science is capitalized in the minds of a few experts. Cannot this treasure be so simplified as to be conveyed to the minds of those who use its practical applications, awakening intellectual response in them? Cannot the story of inventions be so treated as to make the man who manipulates the machine aware of the brain power that is stored up in the machine?

Again, the fine arts in their best period were rooted in the handicrafts—drew from them, their vital sap. Do we not desire that this relation between the artist and the artisan shall be reestablished, to the advantage of both?

But, above all, a human being is endowed with will. A really human being is distinguished from a slave in so far as he exercises his will. Cannot the will of all the different workers be so united that each shall retain its character as an independent factor, while adding its distinctive increment to the resultant total will?

Industrial representation would make the beginning of such a development in the direction of the organic ideal. Industrial representation, indeed, may mean much or little. It may be favored by some as a method to quell the unrest of the manual workers; it may be demanded by the manual workers as a defense against encroachment—the lowering of wages, the lengthening of hours of work—or as a means of correcting Obviously bad conditions. But it may also have the immense significance of being the first step toward the real organization of one of the great social group, the group engaged in industry.[9]

The council of a great industry would include all the functionaries that are factors in it. The main objects would be three:

1. The basic material object of furnishing the product in the requisite quantity and quality.

2. The fixing of salaries, regulated by the rule that the income shall be sufficient to support the worker, whatever his task, in the best possible performance of it.[10]

3. The true ideal object is the promoting of action and reaction between the minds and wills of the different functionaries. Adult education would here have a great role to play. The mind of one worker is to strike sparks of intellectual fire from out the minds of his fellow workers. Even the humblest of them could be intellectually energized by contact with the more gifted. The higher and highest functionaries in turn would gain by the constraint placed upon them of so ripening their thought as to make

it apt for assimilation by the mentally less fortunate. Some mental life slumbers in every brain; some stream of intellectual life is latent in every man. There is no greater test of high intellectual ability than that of performing the miracle of the prophet, that of striking the unpromising rock and drawing living water from it. In general it is my belief that what is miscalled the democratic relation in industry, as in every other sphere, is really not a relation between persons on the same level, but between those on a higher level, and those on a lower level, and that those who are on a higher level can only maintain themselves where they are by the constant effort to draw upward those on the lower level.

The adult education of the workers, besides dealing with the science that is enshrined in the processes, the machinery, etc., should seek to give to the worker as a member of the industrial group, a knowledge of the raw material with which he deals, a knowledge of the countries from which the raw material is drawn, of the people of those countries, their manners, their, customs, their psychology. Adult education should give to the workers a knowledge of the social and economic history of his industry as a whole, not only of the labor movement, and especially of the effects of industry and commerce, on religion and government, in fact, on all the main activities of mankind.[3]

---

[15] The words "organic" and "organization" have become vulgarized in common usage. Organization has almost come to mean no more than association. Any mass of men held together in the most mechanical fashion is nowadays called an organization. It would be helpful to coin a word like "metorganic" on the model of metempirical and metaphysical, to denote the sublime relation to which I have constantly referred in the text. The principle which is the basis of the reconstructed spiritual ideal I am presenting might then be briefly designated as the *rnetorganic* principle, in contrast to the individualistic, the socialist!', etc.

A curious phenomenon may here also be noticed by the way, namely, that the notion of organism has been freely used by precisely the most pronounced individualists. The Stoic is an individualist, but Marcus Aurelius makes a special point of reminding us that what is good for the swarm is good for the bees, and that we are as eyes and ears and hands to one another. The Christian ethic is intensely individualist, but from the Christian scripture comes to us the dictum that we are members of one another. And again Herbert Spencer, in his philosophic writings, constantly makes use of the notion of organism, although few have gone to greater length in asserting the individualistic position than he. The explanation is stimulating and the detrimental effects—and who, in the stint of years g-anted him to work in, seeks to enhance the one and to correct the others. Science, art, as well as trade and industry, have in the main thus far been single track pursuits, intent each on its own special object, drawing indeed on other lines of work, laying them under contribution, but

In the next place, the great council of an industry would care for the recreation of the workers, and in this connection the development in them of the appreciation of beauty —beauty in lines, colors, sounds, and also in the forms of human intercourse. Among the types of recreation would doubtless be instrumental and vocal music, exercises in rhythmic movement, pageants, plays and the like. The purpose of recreation/ however, is not merely to amuse, but to re-create, to renew the spontaneity, the zest, the capacity of the workers for vital working. And if this is granted, then greater attention ought to be given than at present to the kind of recreation which is suited to the different vocations. The art of unbending has been too little

---

not primarily concerned with their effect on the rest. Thus science, in the pursuit of scientific aims, has injured the religious interests of mankind, just as religion at one time injured science; thus commercialism, the pursuit of trade for the sake of the extension of trade, is to-day threatening civilization in its dearest concerns.

3 But there is a lion in the path, a huge obstacle is in the way, of the spiritual penetration of work—it is the blunting uniformity of machine tending. In agriculture this is not equally the case. In it the connection of the hand work with biology, chemistry, etc., is close. Agricultural work is becoming more and more a liberal pursuit. For the mass of

3 *See* the previous chapter.

studied. The lawyer employs certain faculties to excess, so does the business man, so does the clergyman, etc. What kind of recreation then does each need to redress the balance? Plato carefully scrutinized the various kinds of music, with a view to determining the influence they exercise on the minds of those whom he would charge with the rulership of the state, favoring some melodies and eliminating others. The task that Plato assumed for one vocational group should be taken up for all the groups. In our modern cities every kind of music, fiercely passionate, noble, trivial, is offered at random to whoever chooses to come and hear. Plays of every description, fine and bestial, are acted on the open stage without regard even to the age of the spectators. Few are the attempts made to fit the glove to the hand, to give to the mind the peculiar delight in which it is renewed. Industrial representation, no longer confined to the rough problems which it now encounters, will have this task, among others, set for it, that

of solving the problem of furnishing to
the workers the beauty that is ennobling,
the joy that is rejuvenating.

But the central thought in regard to industrial life is still this, that in the delibera-
tions and decisions of the grand council of
an industry, the will of every worker,
whatever his grade of work, shall be
represented; that no one shall be merely, as
Aristotle described the slave, a passive instrument, only just sufficiently human to obey
the commands of a superior, but shall have
his due part in originating the decisions to
which he is subject. Not indeed that he shall
merely put his will into the pool to fight
it out with the other wills, but rather that by
contact and comparison his will may be modified and enlightened, and enter, thus modified and enlightened, into the resultant
united will, he himself being ethicized in the
process.

Finally, the council of the industry should
particularly concern itself with the training
of apprentices, those to whom the torch is

to be handed on, who are to be the successors
of the present generation of workers. For
nothing is so apt to give distinctness to the
ideals of a vocation as the sense of responsibility on the part of those who are engaged
in it to transmit those ideals to the next com-
ers on the scene, and to make the success-
sors more fit and more devoted in the pursuit of them. If any one asks himself:
What kind of man do I desire him to be who
will carry on my work after me? he will find
that his own sense of its significance, its
wide bearings, its worth will thereby be im-
measurably augmented.

I said farther back that I am submitting a
principle and not a scheme. The above suggestions on the method of applying the principle are by way of illustration only. One
who is not himself an industrial worker, and
only sees the ebb and flow of industrial life
from the outside, may get a certain definite
impression of the direction in which it should
be turned. He can record his sketch of the
wiser plan of things, but it is only the men

who are in immediate touch with the concrete realities of the situation, its enormous difficulties, and it's no less vast possibilities, who finally, using inventiveness and genius combined with ethical inspiration, can definitely devise a workable plan.

My contention is that every social system is based on a principle, latent or overt; that social reconstruction must be based on a principle; that the principle we are to adopt, however slowly it may permeate, is to be tested by its effect, not chiefly in increasing the product, or the enjoyment of the producers, but by its effect on the producers themselves, by its effect in promoting the evolution of the human species toward a loftier type.

My thesis is that neither the principle of individual competition nor that of collectivism, nor that of social service as described, is adequate to pass this test; that work must be considered as an opportunity for the perfecting of the personal relations involved therein; that these personal relations must be spiritual, that is, exemplifying the ideally organic relation;[13] that the supreme task is that of personalizing the depersonalized masses of mankind, and their present depersonalized masters as well.

.

V

SOCIETY OF MANKIND

A FEW preliminary remarks may be in order first on the state.

The word "state" suggests fixity, status, established order, leaving out the idea of living growth.

The alternative word "commonwealth" intimates too pointedly the notion of wealth, or well-being, enjoyed in common.

The word "nation" suggests peculiarity or idiosyncrasy owned at birth. We have to do the best we can with an inadequate vocabulary, developing new meanings out of the old stock as experience forces them on us.

As to "sovereignty," the various social institutions, the family, the vocation, the state, etc., are successive stations through which the individual passes on the way to the acquisition of personality. Sovereignty is not restricted to the state. Every group has a sovereignty of its own. The family is

sovereign within its own precincts. There
are limits within which the relations of husband and wife, of parents and children, are
sacrosanct against outside interference. The
vocational group is or should be sovereign
within its own sphere.[2] So is the state sovereign, and finally there is a precinct within
which the individual in his privacy is supreme
—in respect to the freedom of conscience, for
instance. The sovereignty of the state has
been more in evidence, and has been more
frequently discussed, because it is connected
with the use of force within its borders and
the warding off of force from the outside.
Of this circumstance I shall speak later on.
But in essence the sovereignty of the state
does not differ from that of the other groups.
There are rights and obligations within the state
and against the state. There are rights
and obligations stretching beyond the state.

In the series of groups each anterior group
is orientated toward the succeeding ones,
and cannot be defined without reference to
its spiritually educational work in preparing

its members for entrance into the next following group. The family cannot be defined
without reference to the vocation; the vocation cannot be defined without reference to
the state or nation; and the idea of the nation
cannot be grasped without reference to the
society of mankind, of which the nation is
designed to be spiritually a member.[1]

It has been said recently that a nation cannot be described except as a body of people
who believe themselves to be one. But surely
it ought to be possible^ to get beneath this
surface description.

The idea of civilization is the[2] fundamental,
clarifying factor to be here introduced.
Every nation represents a certain type of
human civilization. Its unity consists in this,

---

[1] So far is it from being true that state sovereignty necessarily excludes the idea of the supersovereignty of mankind
that, on the contrary, the conception of the state falls into
hopeless errors whenever that ulterior destination is left out
of sight.

[1] We distinguish between vulgarity and immorality. Vulgarity, as a rule, refers to manners, and not to morals. The
most unprincipled man of the world, the most heartless cynic,
provided he is refined in manner, would not be classed as an
uncivilized person.

its type. Other nations have produced and are producing unlike types of civilization. The society of mankind is the organization in which these different types are to be assembled, in which each is to play its functional part in evoking from the others their best possible contributions to the ulterior perfection of civilization. The ideal of the perfect civilization is the *vinculum societatis humanee,* and supplies that overarching end which is necessary to overcome the friction and clashes of the nations with one another. But is the term "civilization" large enough, wide enough, deep enough, exalted enough, to carry this significance?

What is civilization and who is a civilized being? Civilization is commonly taken to mean the sum total of the things that distinguish the life of men, say in the twentieth century, from that of primitive tribes. Populous cities, no longer holes in the rocks or lake dwellings, swift transportation facilities, the use of electrical power and the like, together with certain acquired knowledges and skills, are reckoned among the factors of civilization. A civilized being, then, would be one who has the advantage of such external conditions, and who in some degree, participates in the sciences and arts of his generation. In addition the notion of civilization applies to manners. Civilized society and polite society are well-nigh synonymous expressions. Uncivilized deportment is such as befits the *vulgus* or crowd, and is out of place in a *civitas,* in a society subject to such refined customs as possess the prescriptive force of laws.

But it must be confessed that the connotation of civilized has not hitherto been conspicuously ethical.[4] And this for two reasons: the one, that the word civilization suggests the public aspect of life, the conveniences and commodities with which that life is furnished, the external polish and glitter of human intercourse, while the term "ethical" refers to the inner worth of men, which has not hitherto been deemed capable of expression in public life, in business or in politics. The second reason is that under the influence of Christianity, the *civitas terrestris,* which is the vehicle and the embodiment of civilization, has been set in opposition to the *civitas superna,* which represents the ideal of a society ethically desirable, ethically perfect. Antagonism has thus been deemed to exist between civilisation and spirituality. Many a Christian has believed that to be ethical or spiritual he must turn his back on civilization and all its works. But if one takes the point of view which I am here submitting, if one thinks of the different groups as stations on the way to personality, if one regards the larger groups, owing to their more complex internal and external relations, as offering-enhanced opportunity for the application of the spiritual rule—that of eliciting- the best in others and thereby in oneself—if one thinks of finite conditions as the raw material on which the spiritual nature of man is to leave its imprint, then civilization may well stand, must stand, for the highest expression of the infinite spirit in the finite human world; and then it at once follows that there is as yet no civilized society, but only a society in the process of becoming civilized; that there is as yet no civilized nation, but only nations in process of becoming civilized; that there is as yet no civilized man, but only men in the way of becoming civilized.

From this standpoint we can now speak of a collective, unitary task of mankind, and the idea of this task furnishes the uniting principle of the world society, or the international society. The task of humanity is to build up a genuine civilization, a *corpus spirituale* of mankind, a counterpart, however incomplete, of the infinite spiritual society, a *civitas terrestris* reflecting the *civitas superna.*

And each nation, as an organic member of this *corpus spirituale,* is to offer its contribution toward the fulfillment of the one all-

embracing task. How? Each nation represents a certain type of the imperfect
civilization which already exists. In the
more advanced nations the type is more explicit. In the more advanced nations it is
possible to see this type mirrored, in its
laws, in its literature, in the acts and the emo-
tions which constitute its political history,
in its manners and customs, in its religion.®
It is impossible to contemplate the mind of
the French people, the English mind, the
German mind, the Russian mind, the Italian
mind, without becoming aware of the irreducible intellectual, sesthetical and volitional
differences that mark them off.[3]

Each of these types has its excellences and
its serious faults, its qualities and its defects.
Every people, prompted by its collective sel-

---

[3] A famous Roman dictum is: "Homo sum; nihil humanum
a me alienum puto" (I am a man, and nothing human do I
consider foreign to me). National conceit ridicuously transr
poses the order of the words in this dictum: "Homo sum;
nihil a me alienum humanum puto" (I am *the* man, and nobody
who is unlike myself do I consider to be quite up to the
human standard).

fishness, its vanity or its pride, is prone to exaggerate its excellences, and to ignore or indulgently tolerate its own faults. Territorial aggrandisement, the desire to possess the earth and the fullness thereof, the spirit of domination, are rationalized by an inveterate national conceit. The Germans sing their futile song: "An deutschem Wesen soli die Welt genesen" (The German way shall heal a world astray). The French, at the outbreak of the great revolution, determined that their ideal of Liberty, Equality and Fraternity should sweep the European continent, and Napoleon's despotism was the outcome. The White Man's Burden, invented by Anglo-Saxon pride, is a burden laid on the brown man's shoulders. And so it goes the world over.

The forces that have produced the international chaos, the cupidities, the racial antipathies, underneath them all the primitive ferocities, would not be as effective for mischief as they are, were they not supported and rationalized by national conceit—the conceit consisting in the one-sided emphasis of the excellences, with no attention paid to and no humility bred by, the corresponding faults. To transform national conceit into something better is the problem. And if once the spiritual relation between the great groups of nations were envisaged, the problem would at least advance toward its solution. This does not mean that we are to attempt to abolish national self-consciousness. We should teach in our schools, emphasize in our histories, the acts of our people and the qualities that are behind the acts which are to their credit; but we should give to our people also the more complete self-knowledge; not hushing up or glossing over the errors they have committed. in the past—yes, their crimes. For there is not a so-called civilized people whose record does not contain the stain of actual crimes such as must bring the blush of shame to a lover of his country. Make your nation realize the urgent need of self-purification, and point the way. The way is that of positive progress toward the perfection of one's national type, the continuous enhancement of its noble and excellent traits." And the method of achieving this result is to follow the spiritual rule. Help to elicit the best in other nations, and thereby in thine own. This practically means to study the types of the sister nations, to consider what are the more excellent traits which they possess, to seek as far as possible to assimilate these, and thus to put oneself in the position of being able to correct their faults, to strengthen them where they are weak, while in the process of so doing, the evil traits in one's own type will gradually diminish and tend to disappear. The German possesses *Grundlichkeit* (thoroughness) in which Americans are deficient. Politically the Germans are deficient in the sense of collective responsibility. The value put on the expert is excessive. The control of the expert by the general public is too feeble. In America the force of the mass is excessive; the influence, in government, of the expert, of exceptional personality that stands out above the mass, is too feeble. America should assimilate the German virtue o: *Gruridlichkeit,* and give in return its own virtue of collective control.

The West in its relations to the East affords a similar illustration of the point I am laboring. The West excels in science, in the mechanical arts, in all that pertains to the expression of the mind along the paths of activity. The East excels in dignity, in deep, detached contemplation. The West has done infinite harm to the East by forcing upon it its alien gifts unmodified, unrelated to the types of civilization which it invaded. Western civilization, western ideas, threaten to undermine the solidarity feeling in Japan, threaten the ancestral piety of the Chinese. The blind Conceit that pushes toward the imperialistic domination of one's own type is wrecking the dearest spiritual possessions of vast families of men.[4]

---

[4] The ideal which I present rests on the recognition of types of civilization and their reciprocal perfection through inter-action, In the more advanced nations the type is clearly recognisable; among other nations the type has become stationary,

The ideal I have sketched is sufficiently far off. When we take up any morning newspaper, we constantly read of new aggressions, new acts Of international violence— the hydra of imperialism puts forth new heads whenever a single one has been cut off—and We are apt, with a sinking of the heart, to ask ourselves whether the far vision of a *corpus spirituale* of mankind is anything more than an idle dream. Still, to ask this question is the unpardonable treachery. To distrust the moral ideal is to doubt that which we have found most certain where we are able to test it in inner experience. And we must not forget that even a plan of behavior between national groups which sa-

---

relatively petrified; among the backward peoples a distinctive type is yet to be developed. It should be the main business of a union of civilized nations to lend its spiritual assistance especially to the child peoples of the earth, beholding in them the depositaries of a treasure, as yet latent, but capable of enriching mankind.

[4] Peace cannot be insured, either economic peace or international peace, unless its terms be such as. right reason and the moral nature of men approve of. Submission on the other hand can be obtained by *force majeure;* though the duration of submission, when gained by subjection, is precarious. Lord Cromer, in his instructive book on "Imperialism," roundly declares that none of the Western nations, neither the Eng-

vors of real morality has never yet been
proposed, except in the vaguest and most in-
effective language.

> "Without the truth there is no knowing;
> Without the way there is no going"

says Thomas a Kempis. First we must
grasp the truth; must propose an ideal
which, if it were turned into reality, would
satisfy our moral nature. But without the
Way there is no going; and the urgent question is, assuming that we begin to see the
goal, what is the next step to be taken in
that direction? How shall we go? How
shall we direct mankind along that way?
What can actually be done?

Much can be done by what is technically
called education—in the schools and col-
leges, for instance, by exhibiting the portraits of the various national minds. As has
been said, the French mind, when compared
with the English, or the German mind,
or the Russian mind, stands out distinctly
enough. A modern French philosopher, Al-

fred Fouillee, has delineated the mind of his own people with the most exemplary intention of impartiality. Again the German mind, with its plus and minus traits (as we may designate them), its attractive and its repellent qualities, stands our distinctly enough, as it is objectively exhibited in German law, German literature, German history, German music, etc. And the same is true of other national minds. One of the obvious methods of promoting education for humanity is to introduce into schools and universities a "science of nations," a knowledge of other nations and the types they represent, along with national self-knowledge. Chief stress should be put on the excellent traits of other peoples, with a view of engendering appreciation as the starting point. Love in the spiritual sense, not peace or prosperity, or even justice, is the bond that is competent to combine the peoples of the earth in unity. "Thou shalt love thy neighbor as thyself," is a commandment that applies to nations as well as to individuals.

But such education as can be given in the lower and higher schools is but a small part of real education which can only be acquired in and by practice. Nations as well as children must learn by doing. In other words, there must be institutions which shall facilitate such contact between peoples as will enable them to understand one another, both to admire and in the deeper sense to compassionate one another. For the evil traits in other nations should provoke compassion, even as the evil life of the publican and the sinner provoked compassion in the founder of Christianity; while indignation, and a certain impatience of evil had better be reserved by each people for its own badnesses.

In the light of these considerations, I shall now proceed to a brief examination of that League of Nations which was created at the close of the recent war, and which has since been the subject of ardent debate between its supporters and opponents. I do not ask: Does the plan of the League realize the ideal of a society of mankind? No one, I imagine, would make such a claim for it. Is it a beginning in the right direction?

Certain advantages may at once be conceded to it. On its administrative side it lends itself to admirable achievements. In such matters as the abolition of the white-slave traffic and of the opium traffic, in securing planetary cooperation to prevent the spread of those terrible pestilences that decimate the populations of the earth by millions, also in international cooperation for scientific research, and a much more difficult undertaking, in putting restrictions on the exploitation of labor. Cooperation of any kind has an educative value. Those who work together where there is no divergence of opinion or interest, are in a better frame of mind to attack those more "thorny" questions in respect to which interests and opinions deviate.

A world court to decide justiciable cases, those cases, namely, in which the gain from a settlement of any kind outweighs the loss to be sustained by an adverse settlement, is no less a distinct step in advance.

But when we face the nonjusticiable cases, those in which what is called national honor, national sovereignty, questions of supreme national interest, are involved, in respect to which each nation reserves to itself the right of independent decision without appeal, we come to the real crux both of the present and of future situations. Is the League competent to deal with such questions? They are the war breeders. The world is weary of war. The prospect of new wars, to be waged with far more frightful instruments of destruction, is not remote, but ominously near. Does the League offer a safeguard against a renewal of such horrors, Or is it a feeble reed likely to break at the very moment when men lean upon it? Will it prevent wars? Or, if it encourages in us a false reliance, will it not on the contrary only serve to bring the danger nearer?

The vulnerable spot of the League, as at present constituted, is, as I see it, that it attempts, after all, to fight the devil with fire; in other words, that it relies on force. It is a league to enforce peace. The bare juxtaposition of the two words, Force and Peace, is paradoxical. It is possible to enforce submission—impotent, abject submission—at least for a time, but peace is a state of mind. It is not possible to enforce a state of mind. The real problem is how to produce the peace-ensuring state of mind in the nations. The whole issue is shifted from its proper base when the sword is once more evoked to end the use of the sword. The League as designed is a league to force submission, not to ensure peace.[8]

The misleading analogy drawn from the example of domestic courts of justice serves to confuse the debate. Did not the courts, it is said, put an end to the private feuds, the quarrels between individual and individual? Why, then, should not a court put an end to the quarrels of nations, thus ruling out the class of nonjusticiable cases entirely, making all questions justiciable? A misleading analogy is one in which the points of likeness are stressed, the high light thrown upon them, while the points of difference are slighted or ignored.[5] But the difference is immense between the quarrels of nations and private quarrels. In the case of attacks on the life and property of individuals, and in civil cases as well, the rights of the parties concerned are in the main known and acknowledged. The general principles are laid down. New law is indeed made from time to time, but the new law moves along the lines previously laid down. That a man's life shall be immune against violence, that his property shall be safe against theft, that contracts shall be kept, etc., are matters on which the conscience of mankind is made

---

[5] The craving of the average man for the simplification of complex problems leads to the construction of such misleading anadogies. The average man has come to realize the folly of war. He is weary of war. He sees that humanity has run into a kind of impasse. In his impatience he insists on some short-cut way out. The analogy of the court and the policeman's club is just apparently simple enough to meet his views. But there is no short-cut way to peace, peace being a state of mind. In general it _ may be said that the tendency to undue simplification on difficult questions is one of the principal obstacles to real progress. It constantly leads men off on false scents, and into bypaths from which they must eventually retrace their steps.

up. The nonjusticiable cases that arise between the nations, on the other hand, relate to matters on which the conscience of mankind is *not yet made up,* is still in process of formation. The analogy, therefore, does not fit. Who shall say when the life of a nation is threatened? Is Germany killed when certain parts of Silesia are taken from her? Was France killed when she was deprived of Alsace and Lorraine in 1871? Who shall say when a nation has been robbed of its property? What, in fact, is its property? What are the boundaries to which it is entitled to lay claim? And how far has it such other rights as access to the sea, or to raw materials, such as rubber or oil and the like, in distant countries, in the tropics, in Asia? Or, again, what are the real rights of minorities, such, as of the Czechs in Bohemia when the Germans were in control, or of the Germans now that the Czechs are in control, or of the Slovaks as against the Czechs? What are the rights of majorities as against the ruling minorities,

as in India? In regard to all such questions
as these, there is still wide disagreement,
even among those who desire only that justice shall be done, let alone those who are
governed by less reputable motives. What
I am calling attention to is that the dissimilarity between the feuds of nations and the
feuds of private individuals is parallel to the
dissimilarity between those cases where the
conscience of mankind is made up, and those
other more numerous cases where the conscience of mankind is not yet made up is indeed
only in the early stages of formation.[6]

To intrust the decision of the latter species of cases to a court would have a further
inconvenience in that the judicial mind is
apt to lean backward in the direction of
precedents, as it properly may where the
rights of the parties are known; and that

---

[6] It is also of great importance to observe that the rights
of individuals depend on the principle of likeness, relating, as
they do, to matters in respect to which all human beings are
alike. All human beings ought to be treated as having iden-
tical claims, while the rights of groups, both internal, and external, depend on the principle of unlikeness, or the differen-
tiation of functions,

it is therefore scarcely the suitable kind of mind to deal with *unprecedented* situations such as are constantly arising in international intercourse.

One further consideration may be added: in deciding between individuals, two indispensable precautions are taken by the courts— the one, an elaborate system of procedure to sift the evidence, the other, regulations to secure the impartiality of judges. Among the most important of the latter is the pro vision that those persons to-whom judgment is intrusted shall not themselves be parties in interest. This has no difficulty in the case of a controversy affecting any A and B, since there are millions of fellow citizens who have no personal interest in A and B or their concerns; but in the case of nations the situation is absolutely different. Half a dozen nations rule the roost to-day in this world of ours. The smaller nations are dependent more or less on the good will of the more powerful. There is not a serious case of dispute, therefore, that can come up in the world court in which the judges themselves are not directly or' indirectly interested on one side or the other. The ind.spensable safeguard of impartiality is lacking.'

Finally, to return to the question of the use of force, it may be said, I think without fear of contradiction, that the force used by the courts is in essence not physical but moral force. The few thousand officers of police who maintain order in a great city would be powerless to do so did not the moral sense of the community support them. Yes, it is the moral sense of the community that must also find ts echo in the mind of the offender against the law, and bring him, morally speaking, to his senses. Where this is not the case and mere force is used to subjugate the offender, the administration of justice is still barbarous. The object of all punishment, as modern penology recognizes, is not to break the will of the criminal, not to subject him to the *force majeure* of society, but to produce in him a state of mind apt to make for social peace. Mere repression, even in the domestic administration of justice, is out of date. To use this antiquated method as an argument for mere repression by a league of nations would be deplorable. There are then nonjusticiable cases (let us face this fact), cases in which the conscience of mankind is not yet made up. *The immediate aim of an incipient society of mankind must be to devise methods by which the formation of a world conscience may be accelerated.* One of these methods would be international conferences devoted to some single, urgent issue on which public opinion could be focused, like the recent Washington Conference for Naval Disarmament. The distractedness of public opinion, due to the great variety of interests which in kaleidoscopic succession claim its attention, disables public opinion from exerting its proper influence. Public opinion at present is said to govern. But, in fact, public opinion is constantly baffled, rendered uncertain, hesitant and, save at rare moments, impuissant, by the dizzy diversity of objects toward which it is in turn directed. The concentration of public opinion is the *sine qua, non* of its effectiveness. There is as yet no world public opinion. It has to be created. The authentic publicity of the discussions that would take place in such an international conference is equally indispensable in order to thwart the insidious arts of prejudiced propaganda.

The members of the international conference, however, should include not only the diplomatic agents of government, but delegations, elected by the parliaments, representing labor, commerce, and all the social groups. The people who would suffer by the outbreak of war should be present in their delegates in the conference that is intended to prevent it.

At a critical juncture, when war is imminent, the conference should be summoned and the confrontation of the parties concerned, in the midst of an international body, where the plea coming from either side could be sifted, would be in order. The Germans at the beginning of the late war were diligent enough in spreading their case broadcast in every country which they could reach; so were the Allies. But the situation would have been quite different if each had been compelled to present its side in the presence of the other side, not before a council of ambassadors or of diplomats, but in the presence of a body actually representing the world. Each side not being permitted one-sidedly to overstate its own case, would then have been compelled to meet the arguments of its adversary and then, with the eyes of mankind upon them, the specious pretensions by which each covered the motives it did not dare to confess would have been stripped off; they would have been challenged to show the actual rightfulness of their pretensions or to suffer world condemnation.[7]

---

[7] It may be said that without any such confrontation the judgment of the world went against Germany, and that Germany at the Peace of Versailles, subscribed to the confession of her own exclusive guilt. But this was notoriously done under duress, and has not created in the German people the state of mind that makes for international peace. And the sentence passed by the world was really passed by those who were the convinced opponents of Germany. As to the sole guilt of the latter country, this verdict has been modified by numerous revelations that have since appeared.

But I find myself in danger of passing into details that lead off from the main object with which I am here concerned. That object is to find a principle which, if men can be educated up to it, however long the process of education may take, will triumph over the antisocial tendencies that rage between nations at present, and that will serve as the lasting basis of a society of mankind. Is the League of Nations founded on such *a principle*?

The principle on which the League is founded is respect for the equal rights of strong and weak nations. This is the idealistic element in it which fascinated men when the plan of the League was first announced; And when the covenant of the League failed to answer the expectations that had been raised, disappointment was proportionately severe, and the expression was often heard that idealism had gone down to defeat. This pessimistic inference, however, is not warranted. For, aside from the practical obstacles that always stand in the way of the immediate realization of an ideal, it must be acknowledged that the ideal itself, as presented, and still urged, is imperfect in a vital particular.

The equal rights of weak and strong nations are affirmed on ethical grounds. To this we assent. But when we press the inescapable question—equal right to what? the answer is by no means satisfactory. Equal right, we are informed, to self-determination; a right which, unless promptly qualified, proves mischievous, bringing international anarchy in its train. But qualified how, on what grounds? To this in the ideal of the League there is no answer. Again, what is the object for the sake of which self-determination is to be accorded to each nation? Answer, in order that it may work out its happiness, its prosperity, unhindered by its neighbors. But this is an appeal to enlightened self-interest, and is by no means an ethical appeal. And, moreover, has it not been demonstrated many times over that it is not in the nature of self-interest to be enlightened; that self-interest when interpreted to mean the satisfaction of the desires of the self, always grasps at immediate satisfactions as soon as the opportunity of obtaining them is sufficiently tempting? It may be said that in the long run it is really to the interest of the strong to refrain from aggression against the weak. But when have the strong ever been deterred from violence against the weak by the consideration of what is best in the long run? It might have been better for the world, it assuredly would have been, if there had not been the scramble for the spoils of Africa; it might have been better for Russia to have resisted the temptation to seize Port Arthur, and for Germany to have refrained from seizing Kiau Chiau, etc.; it might have been better for Italy not to have laid hands on Tripoli—only to mention a few of the occurrences which have already been superseded by more recent acts of aggression, perpetrated, indeed, by members of the League themselves, since the League was formed.

To tie the nations together in the bond of amity and unity by the tie of self-interest, is to tie them with a rope of sand, is to bind them with green withes, like those with which Samson was bound, flimsy fetters which the war giant will snap as soon as it occurs to him to rise up in his brutal strength.[8]

The principle of equal rights for the weak and the strong is sacred. Even to enunciate it at all, however untenable the grounds on which it was put, may prove profitable to the human race. In so far our judgment of the League will be favorable.[9] But another and a

---

[8] As the use of repressive force by the League is an application of an obsolete method of punishment, so the glittering ideal of the League is merely an application to the nations of the obsolete individualistic philosophy of the eighteenth century, which has been tried and been found wanting in the competitive, -internal, economic relations. To encourage men, whether as individuals or as nations, to put forth their utmost efforts in an attempt selfishly to gain material happiness, and at the same time to require that they respect the equal selfishness of their fellows, is to ask them to follow contradictory motives.

renounce the policy of repression by the force which it embodies. In the sixteenth century the seamen of many countries were obstinately determined to find a Northwest Passage to the Indies. They tapped the American continent at various points. It is pathetic, for instance, to think of Hendrick Hudson sailing up the river which bears his name in the expectation of reaching the ocean beyond, unaware of the three thousand miles of land

sounder   foundation   must   be   found—
not peace for the sake of prosperity, not an
equal right to the vague thing called national
happiness, can we, at least from the spiritual
point of view, approve, but rather an equal
right for each people to contribute its best
toward the fulfillment of the task of mankind, an equal right to perfect that type of
civilization for which it stands, with the view
of perfecting the greater and nobler civilization of the future." An intrinsic bond only,
can finally unite the peoples of the earth.
And that intrinsic bond is not self-interest,
but (if the expression be allowed) international love, the love that acknowledges that
the best in the life of other peoples is an
essential element in a people's own best life,
and that a nation produces the best in itself
by endeavoring to bring the deposit of the

---

that interposed between the headwaters of the river and the Pacific. At last they gave up the fruitless search for a North-west Passage. Magellan rounded the southern cape, and in our day the great continental wall was pierced at Panama. The League is at least a good beginning so far as its ostensible purpose is concerned, but as to the way by which it seeks to accomplish its purpose it is a bad beginning.

best in others to light.

The guiding thoughts which have been followed in this exposition are:

1. The spiritual rule as enunciated is applicable alike in the family, in the vocation, in the state, in international relations.

2. Whatever constitution for an international society may be proposed is to be tested and judged by the ennobling retroactive effect it is likely to have on the member nations themselves.

3. In order to overcome the clash of interests and purposes, there must be an overarching end, an end so commanding and august that the private interests are seen to be best achieved when they strip themselves of their privacy and coincide with that ulterior, grander end. In the case of the "clash of nation with nation, the overarching end is the spiritual ideal of civilization as defined.

4. For practical next steps toward the formation of a society of mankind, the three thoughts are: concentration on one urgent

issue at a time with a view of gradually creating an enlightened world public opinion; confrontation in the case of controversies with the view of overcoming *ex parte* propaganda and bringing out the right on either side, and finally co-relation instead of mere coordination, with the view of helping on the organisation of the *corpus spiritual e,* the civilization in which the soul of humanity will have its body.

Concentration, Confrontation, Co-relation.[10]

---

which human nature must find its satisfaction.

VI

ATTITUDE TOWARD LIFE

WHAT does it all mean? and, What do I mean in the scheme of things? are the two questions. And the answer implied in the foregoing lectures is: I must find out what I mean, and then I shall know what the world means. The key of the secret is in my own bosom. Philosophers have in vain tried the opposite procedure, constructing a metaphysical picture of the world, and then finding a place for man in it. I find a way out of my own perplexities by starting with, by trying the ethical approach, by searching for a point where the infinite appears in human nature itself, that is, in ethical experience, and from that point building up the eternal world, enveloping my spiritual nature with the infinite company of spiritual beings related to it.

The decisive turn is taken in the equations: ethical quality equals worth; worth equals indispensableness; indispensableness equals membership in an ideal infinite Organism, a *corpus spirituale.* The essential spiritual nature of man is not atomistic, but social, or rather, suprasocial. ⸱ In his inmost Self man is related to other selves, in such fashion that he lives in them and they in him.

What, then, is it that makes life worth while? What the prize for which the race is to be run? What my sovereign end? What the object which above all others it imports that I seek to attain? It is the conviction, through the experience of the spiritual nature in myself, that the ultimate reality in things is spiritual, that there is an eternal order in which I, in the ultimate truth of my being, am inseparably included; that the world is not a madhouse, though with its cruelties it often seems such; that a human being is not a mere wave of the flux, though the days of his life be but threescore years and ten, and full of sorrow and trouble.

In a word, the prize for which the arduous race is to be run by me is the conviction that I have a soul—to use for a moment the familiar word, despite its uncanny connotations. The conviction that man has a soul is not a gratuitous boon, a gift bestowed on him by fairy hands at his cradle; it is not to be believed on hearsay or on the authority of some revelation; it is a prize to be won by hard, assiduous effort continued through a lifetime, and becoming surer for those who do not relax the effort as they approach the end.

Self-knowledge then in the sense of knowledge that penetrates down to the essence of the self, is the supreme aim. But self-knowledge, be it distinctly noted, for the sake of the illumination it casts on the world, the cosmic inferences it permits and necessitates; self-knowledge, whereby to overcome the sense of alienness that so deeply troubles us as subsisting between the world and ourselves; self-knowledge as a means of making our peace with the universe, of making it a home.

Now, in order to know oneself as a spiritual being, it is necessary to see others as spiritual beings. The *conditio sine qua non* for one who seeks to learn the spiritual attitude toward life is to acquire the power of second-sight, the clairvoyance that will enable him to see his fellow human beings, despite their repulsive traits, their often hideous imperfections, as potential spiritual companions. For to know the self is to know it in its relations, is to know it as exercising a distinctive kind of energy on others.[1]

How, then, shall one acquire this excellent art of clairvoyance, of spiritual second-sight; how shake oneself free of the insistent impressions made on the mind by the actual behavior of others, by that outside nature of theirs, if indeed it be the mere

---

[1] To speak of self-knowledge in any other sense would be misleading. The self as it exists in the eternal order is incognisable, and unimaginable. What we predicate of it is distinctiveness, and the relation of joint action and reaction, of energy projected and energetic impact received, that subsists between it and an infinity of other spiritual beings. It is by thus defining it in terms of the ideal organism that we have taken the third step in definition, in advance of the vague holiness definition of the Hebrews and the atomistic conception of Christianity. _ (Cf. chapter 2.) The word spiritual means for us simply ideally organic.

outside, which in any case is so hard to penetrate? Starting from the legitimate presupposition that the constitution of the mind
is fundamentally the same in all men, that
certain fundamental experiences of mine are
capable of being experienced by others,[2]1 begin by attributing to my fellowmen the same
distinction between body and mind which I
am aware of in myself. Here the Stoic
teaching can be of use. Following Epic-
tetus we can say: If there is a pain in thy
limb, remember that the pain is in thy limb
and not in thee; if in leprosy or some other
horrible disease the; body become a mass of
festering sores; if in the last stages of ill-
ness the physical part of thee is about to
crumble into dust, remember that this putrid
thing is not thou; that the little heap of
dust which presently is all that will remain of
the: physical part of thee is after all
not the whole thing, not the essential thing,
not thou. But if this is true of thee, it

[2] It will presently be seen that this does not conflict with
the unlikeness which has been emphasized throughout these
lectures.

is true also of thy fellow. Apply to him the same discrimination between that which is not his real self and that which is. Even though at the outset you know nothing of the latter, in any case there *is* something that is not the bodily part. That is a fair starting point.

. I proceed next, helped in my search for selfhood by the Hebrew-Christian teaching, to distinguish between that which is morally evil in me, that which yields to the persuasion of the grosser appetites, of the anti-social passions and the like, and that other thing in me which is competent to resist those impulsions and solicitations. Perhaps I find that my own deflections from the standard of what I conceive to be right are not as crass as those of some others. I am neither a criminal nor sodden in drink, and yet in my own eyes I am not a whit less culpable, possibly more so, than those whose heredity was darker, whose advantages were less. Nevertheless, I know that whatever errors I may have committed, there is in me an inexhaustible potency of regeneration. There never is a moment when I can not turn over a new leaf, when I can not gain from past experience the purchase for a new upward start. This capital experience also I transfer to others. Even though they often have the semblance of ravening beasts I must see them as capable of a moral metempsychosis here and now. The issue between those who are spiritually minded and those who are secular minded is put sharply in the expression "a hopeless case," as I have seen it frequently used, for instance, in the discussion of marriage, it being argued that marriage should be dissolved when the case is hopeless. To the spiritually minded no human being is a mere case, and no human being is hopeless—that is the decisive point of difference. Jesus, in consorting with publicans and harlots, acted upon this divine presupposition. He taught faith and taught it effectually because he had it. We are trying to see others spiritually; how far have we proceeded? I look at a man and

I say to myself: he is not all body; there is something else in him not physical. I look at one who is living in evil ways, and I say he is not sentenced to go on living so wretchedly. There is a power of rejuvenation in him if only it can be reached.

But is it not possible to form a more definite image of the spiritual being in order to counteract the overwhelming impression produced by the outside of men's lives? The ideally organic conception comes to our aid. The spiritual self is apprehended in its energizing. The energizing of a man is particularly conspicuous in his vocation. I can form a definite spiritual image of another when I picture him exercising his vocation according to the spiritual rule. For instance, when I think of a man engaged in business or in industry, I can think of him spiritually as dropping the motive of pecuniary gain and substituting for it the service motive, as explained in chapter four. I can picture a lawyer spiritually when I think of him as exercising his function as a teacher of justice, a mediator and promoter of progressive justice. I can picture a woman spiritually when I think of her as exercising in marriage and the family that solar influence which I have described in the third chapter. And so in all relations, in citizenship, in the relation of the individual through his own nation to other nations. In friendship also the spiritual image is that of the man as he envisages this relation from the point of view of the spiritual rule, as he tries to super-induce upon the bare facts of his relation that spiritual significance which they are capable of engendering. Such spiritual images of friends and spouses, and fellow citizens of my people and of mankind I am to form as I pass through life. I am to be the creator of these spiritual images. And, having these images in mind, so far as I am connected with others, I am to see them in the light of this their possible perfection, and by seeing them and by changing myself, induce them to approximate to their possible perfection.

Every man and woman should thus be a . spiritual artist, portrait painter, the portraits painted having this virtue in them that they are not only like the spiritual original, but that the original, beholding them, is stirred to a great love for this his sublime counter- part, and is moved in some measure to con- form to it.

It will be admitted, I imagine, that the ideal as thus presented is no longer in the air, that it has "hands and feet," that it is capable of coming home to men's business and bosoms, of taking hold of a disorganized world and offering it a principle of organisation, and that it thus becomes possible to pursue jointly the task of external betterment and the improvement of human nature itself. But how far can we succeed in the prosecution of this task? Can we at all expect, under finite conditions, to reach the goal of ethical perfection? Is there to be an ethical millennium? And if not, if we are striving to attain that which finitely is unattainable, what profit is there in striving? What after all is the worthwhile outcome of our endeavors?

The mystics speak of a dark ground in God. The material in nature and in human nature on which we operate is in an ultimate sense intractable to the spiritual pattern which we seek to impose upon it, not wholly intractable indeed, for in the course of ages the propensities inherited by us from the inferior creatures have been in part subdued and modified, and there is hope of a progresses to which no bounds can be set, in an upward direction. Nevertheless, in an ultimate sense human nature as we know it, and the ideal of perfection toward which the mind stretches, can never coalesce.

Again, man, on the natural side of him, is a part of the time and space world; and since time and space though illimitable are not infinite, the time and space world itself can never be rounded into a systematic whole, can never present that completeness which perfection, by the very notion of it, requires. We stand here veritably before an abyss, the abyss that separates the imperfect from the perfect, the finite from the infinite, we face the final question that every world view, every *Weltanschauung*, must somehow reckon with: How, if perfection exists, say in the eternal world, is it possible that imperfection should exist alongside of it? There have been many attempts to bridge this gulf by means of so-called theodicies, which are intended to explain and justify the coexistence. It cannot be justified. Explanation is impossible. To explain is to assign a cause; and causality, or the rule that every antecedent is followed by its appropriate consequent applies within the sequence of phenomena, but does not apply to the relation between phenomena and that which is not phenomenon, the infinite or eternal. Every theodicy has broken down. Every one of them, when closely scrutinized, is seen to contain a fallacy of some kind, and to embarrass the moral sense as well. The Creation hypothesis is the most outstanding example: "And God saw everything that He had made, and behold it was very good." The words "He made" are intended to designate a particular kind of causality, and are liable to the objection just stated, while the optimism conveyed in the phrase "very good," is either so blind or so transcendental that the average moral consciousness is unable to deal with it.

The great philosopher of harmonization, Leibnitz, comes to the assistance of theology by arguing that even if this world is in many ways defective, it is yet the best of all worlds of which the existence was possible. The mathematics of this argument may illustrate the genius of Leibnitz, but the conclusion reached will be cold comfort to those who are crushed by the physical and moral evils of this best possible world. And, besides, there is implied a discouraging reflection upon the power of the Deity. If this was the best possible world, might it not have been better that He should have abstained from creating and remained quiescent in his eternal sanctuary?

The difficulty remains, no matter what the hypothesis. If it be pantheistic, then how can the finite emanate from the infinite; if it be Hegelian absolutism, how can the perfect lapse into the imperfect? How account for the initial lapse? If St. Augustine tells us that the world is to be compared to a picture, and the evils therein to the shadows that serve to bring the lights into relief, we shall summon to witness against him some mother of a dying child, and ask her whether she is satisfied with the explanation that the suffering and death of her beautiful child is a means of bringing into relief the life and happiness of other people's children. Besides, is it true that the lights in the picture, predominate over the shadows? Does not our judgment as to that depend very largely upon temperament? And who is it after all that sees the whole picture? The Deity of the all-seeing eye. And can we imagine that He, like a human beholder, should need those dark shadows in order to enhance His pleasure in the illuminated parts? Oh how fragile, how crumbling are the planks which are used to construct a bridge over the abyss that separates the imperfect from the perfect!

Agnosticism, it seems, would be the way, out, and it is for the secular minded; it cannot be for the spiritually minded. By the phrase secular minded, I intend no imputation. I mean by it those who are content to make themselves and others at home in the world as it is as far as possible, whose wisdom it is to clinch their teeth and to endure the inevitable whenever they and those they care most for, are hard hit, and who regard the ideal as at best a poetic illusion, on a par with creations of the poetic imagination in general. But agnosticism of this kind, I say, cannot be the way out for the spiritually minded, that is, for those who regard the ideal of perfection as the mind's representation of that which actually exists. With this view, agnosticism in a certain sense is indeed compatible. In the sense that we cannot know, if to know means to explain, to assign a cause. But if to know may also mean to be convinced and

that on grounds of immediate experience of
man's worth arid what that worth implies, if
it means the consciousness that one lives in
promoting the life cf another, and recipro-
cally in being awakened to true life by the
effect on oneself of another's life; if this experience, this awareness of reciprocity, of
being at once cause and effect, is a real
experience, then we can rid ourselves of
agnosticism as a final attitude. For then
the spiritual rule, the rule that obtains within
the ideal order, has been verified to us, by the
operation of it in ourselves.

And another thought of vital consequence
needs here to be added. The experience referred to is not one to be wished for or not
as one pleases, as one may desire to become a
great scientist or a great artist, or forego
such ambitions if he prefers. Ethically,
spiritually, every human being is called, and
chosen to be great. For whatever the incon-
ceivable relations between the perfect and
the imperfect may be, this at least is borne
in upon us,—that the infinite presses upon us

to be expressed in our finite experience. Upon the human self there is this pressure from the transcendental world. The acquisition of a high ethical character is not a matter of mere subjective choice, as one often hears it said that he who remains morally undeveloped is one who fails to become acquainted with the eternal values during his brief existence. He misses something which he might have had if he had chosen; he goes without the finest insights which he might have achieved. He is a wave of the flux, but the light of the eternal sun might have shimmered on the crest of his little wave. All this is subjective, while the real ethical experience is that of an objective task to be accomplished, of an experience to be gained, not because it is merely delightful, since it is fraught with pain, but to be gained nevertheless because as finite beings we are subject to the pressure of the eternal world.

It is this that distinguishes the attitude toward life which I have expounded, even from those systems which rate the ethical values as values above all others, whilst still retaining them as values to be appreciated subjectively by the individuals to whom they appeal.

But I must now return to the question raised above. If the perfect realization is impossible in the finite world, if we are bound for a goal which finitely we cannot reach, what is the worthwhileness of our life? What is the outcome of our experience? The outcome is, intense consciousness of the pressure which it is spiritual death to resist. The outcome is the knowledge of that spiritual rule which it is possible for us, within limits, to apply successfully, when and in so far as we succeed in doing so, our relations to fellow human beings become irradiated. Marriage is glorified by the spiritual rule, friendship is; our work in the vocations ceases to be restricted to obvious ends, and acquires a great, yes cosmic significance.

So does our citizenship, and the term "Civilization" is lifted out of its connection with the *civitas terrestris* to become the earthly mirror of the *civitas superna*. There is no lack of incentive to work cheerfully and courageously along spiritual lines in the finite world to which we belong. Every attempt to apply successfully the spiritual rule confirms our confidence in the rule, our consciousness of the existence of a spiritual part in us. And every failure in turn, every frustration of effort, only intensifies our will to renew the effort, only clears and exalts our conception of that majestic infinite which cannot be realized in the finite, because the finite breaks down under its weight.

The ideal which I have enunciated has been accused of overemphasizing frustration, of leading to a depressing view of life. If to stand at the brink, as it were, of the finite, and to look out upon the solemn serenity of the eternal order is depressing, then the accusation is just. But frustration is only the stepping-stone. The accent of my view of

life is on that which lies beyond the frustration—frustration being the inevitable
means to the holiest vision. And for
success, too, I repeat, a place is found in
this ideal, since it is only by a vigorous attack upon the actual, finite relations, with
a view to organising them, that the self-
knowledge of which I have spoken all along
can be achieved.[3]

In the first chapter, entitled "De Profundis," it
was laid down that every great ideal is born of
pain and corresponds to certain urgent
objective needs. Three needs of our time and
generation were mentioned, and three problems
arising out of these needs: the problem of the
insignificance of man in the face of the
innumerable worlds, the problem of the man
who perishes in the meanwhile, and the problem
of the divided conscience.

Nothing has been effectually said in these
chapters if the answer to the first prob-

---

[3] How the evils with which human life is afflicted, how
sickness, guilt and bereavement can be utilized in the interests of spiritual self-knowledge, I have indicated in the third
part of my Ethical Philosophy.

lem is not now evident. The sense of man's utter nothingness is relieved, the heavy pall of the consciousness of insignificance is lifted by self-knowledge—man's knowledge of himself as a spiritual being. Gazing at night upon the star-sown firmament he is not dwarfed into littleness. Stars and suns are lesser lights compared with those supra-solar luminaries that constitute the spiritual universe. And the magnitudes of space and time, far from overwhelming him, are useful as supports to lean on in rising to the conception of the transcendent magnitude of the infinite host of spirits whereof man is one—an infinitesimal one (hence his humility), an indispensable one (hence his dignity).

The solution of the second problem concerning the fate of the man who perishes in the meantime is that spiritually he need not perish in the meantime; he has worth and he can affirm it under no matter what material conditions. His worth demands, indeed, that the conditions under which he lives be incessantly improved, but he is not, the helpless victim of his conditions for all that. He can exercise the spiritual rule of promoting the best in others, his wife and children, for instance, thereby honoring the best in himself, in the meanest hovel of the slums.[4] The problem of the divided conscience—the moral law recognized in the private relations and the law of strife prevailing in business and politics—ceases to exist under the spiritual ideal as stated. There are no longer two laws, the conscience is no longer distracted by opposite tendencies. There is one law, that runs through all the human relations, the family, the vocation, the state, etc. These are successive stages on the road toward the supreme goal. One and the same rule obtains in all, only blossoming into richer meanings as man passes out of the nearer into the more remote— out of the narrower into the wider groups.[5]

---

[4] That the statement in the text is not overstrained is demonstrated by the examples of moral grandeur which are often encountered among the poorest by those who are familiar with their lives.

[5] A distinction, it is true, must be recognized between the nearer groups within which man is relatively independent in

Spinoza has truly said that wisdom consists not in the contemplation of death but
in the contemplation of life. Nevertheless it
is well at times in imagination to think of
oneself as facing death, in order then to turn
back and form a juster estimate of the
aims and ends of life that really count. It
is not too much to say that most men live
provisional lives, absorbed in the pursuit of
merely provisional ends, such as to build up

---

the exercise of influence,' less dependent on the cooperation
of others, and those wider-groups in which, in order to effect
apparent changes, he is dependent on the cooperation of many,
nay of multitudes. The present competitive system, for instance, cannot be abolished by any single employer or small
group of employers, however well-intentioned they may be;
our bad politics cannot be redeemed by a single or a few
high-minded citizens; and still less can the international situation be changed even by an idealistic statesman. There are
clearly limits to the application of the spiritual rule by any
man throughout all the relations in which he stands. He is a
man of affairs, and he cannot of his own motion change the
business habits of the world; he is a citizen, but he cannot
extemporize the noble state; he is a member of mankind, but y
he cannot, through his own unaided efforts, establish the world
society. But two considerations are pertinent: he can do
something in each of these relations to give an impetus in
the right direction, and it is the direction that counts so far –
as he is concerned; and he can, in those groups where he is
relatively competent, apply the potent strength of that spiritual
rule which is the yeast that is competent to leaven the whole
lump—he can kindle a fire that by and by will spread its living
ardor throughout mankind. He can even contribute toward
national peace and justice by extirpating from his own heart
the racial antipathies, the hatreds, the cupidities, that are the
ultimate causes of the vast world discord.

a business, or to carry through a scheme of reform, or to see their children happily married or successful in some profession; and they forget that these same children, now young perhaps, will presently stand where they stand—at the brink—the few decades allotted to human beings passing for them also with incredible swiftness. The activities and the provisional ends seem futile enough unless they are linked to some ulterior ultimate end.

Standing then at the terminus, I should say that one guiding thought for me would be continued interest in the progress of the human race to which I belong. A youth thinks of his mature age as the continuation of his present life, so I think of future generations as continuing my earthly life, and as I desire progress for myself, so I desire it for mankind. Progress means advance toward a society which shall more adequately reflect in all its relations the pattern of the spiritual world. To see God as reflected in the face of Christ is the theological way of putting this idea; to see the world of spiritual perfection as reflected in the face of humanity is the turn I give to the same thought.[6]

And the second crucial thought that touches me is that of the persistence of the spiritual part. Do we live merely in the effect we leave behind upon the life of future generations on this earth? Is the spiritual part of us obliterated? The doctrine of immortality as commonly understood means that the psychophysical organism will continue to exist in some attenuated fashion in another sphere. The departed will be recog-

---

[6] That there actually is progress in human history it is impossible to prove. I rest my belief in progress, not on the fact that it is demonstrable, for it is not demonstrable, but on the moral pronouncement that it ought to be, that therefore it can be, and must be.

I may add that the idea of living in the life of future generations is one thing, that of living in the memory of future generations is quite another thing. The latter has never appealed to me. Some of the greatest benefactors of the race in the past have been forgotten—not even their names have come down to us: Those that are remembered are few in number, and their memory is often disfigured, and their teachings, as in the case of Jesus, distorted. Not to be quite forgotten by those whom we have loved and who love us is a pleasing thought, but they who remember us will in turn soon pass from the scene, and our so-called earthly immortality will die with them. How ironically touching are the inscriptions on tombstones!

nisable, their arms will be outstretched to welcome us, and the like. Or again, the psychic is supposed to be clothed with, to assume (a vague form of speech to which no definable meaning whatever can be attached) new organs unlike - the bodily. These evidently are projections of temporal conditions into the admittedly non-temporal; the last outreachings of human tenderness striving to keep hold of the beloved as a concrete object.

With the doctrine in this version of it I am not concerned. What is required of me is the valiancy of truth. I must train myself to relinquish tranquilly and *in toto* the psychophysical self. What I retain is the conviction that the spiritual self is the eternal self and cannot perish. And secondly, that this spiritual self of mine, being social or suprasocial, is inseparably bound up with other spiritual selves, and in this sense that those I have loved and I, cannot be parted in eternity. And if I seek communion with them while I still live here,

I must produce the best in myself in order to encounter the best in them which is their very being.[7]

THE END

---

[7] The weak spot in the usual arguments for immortality is that the soul or the spiritual part is taken atomistically, not socially. As an individual, or atomic entity, being only an imperfect copy of the individual God, there is no reason why it should continue to exist. Even if it did, since it is not linked up by any necessity with the infinite Deity, it might, for all we know, be set adrift amid the immensities, wandering, as Seneca fancies, among the stars. The doctrine of immortality as thus taught has in consequence dwindled into a mere hope. But the most ardent hope may be disappointed; for hope is a favorable view of what may be but is not certain to be, and is ever attended by its obverse fear.

The social, or suprasocial character of the spiritual part of man, offers a new approach to the problem.

[11] In a parallel course on the idea of culture (delivered alongside the present six Hibbert lectures), I presented the thought that an artisan can be a cultured person as well as a poet or a scholar. He is cultured who realizes the effect produced by his vocation on the other chief vocations—both the

[5] Even where the religion is nominally the same, as among the Christian peoples, there are religious differences that point to characteristic differences in the national genius, the national

lish, nor the French, nor even the Russians, have secured the allegiance of the subject peoples over whom they rule, and he ascribes this to that inveterate repugnance to foreign domination, which is natural to the tribes of men everywhere. One is aware of the heaving and seething of revolt in the East, underneath the crust of Western supremacy.

[11] The Supreme Court of the United States is sometimes cited as an illustration of the kind of superiority to prejudice which may be expected from particularly high-minded men summoned to decide in an international controversy. But the citation is not wholly fortunate if one remembers the action of Supreme Court judges at the time of the Hayes-Tilden election, when it was found at the critical juncture that the distinguished persons whose high-mindedness no one doubted nevertheless followed the bias of their Republican or Democratic affiliation.

[14] Critics of the League are often told that at least a beginning has been made. Let the covenant of the League be amended, but let us not sacrifice what we have gained. A statement of this kind needs to be carefully scrutinized. Is the beginning that has been made a good start? In what respect is it a good start, and in what respect is it a bad start? Fifty-one nations have combined to keep the peace among themselves. The mere setting up of this object is a good beginning, but the way by which it is proposed to accomplish the object is bad—in so far the beginning that has been made is bad. The way along which it is proposed to reach the goal may prove to be not a highway, but a byway, which threatens to end in a bog. It may be, therefore, necessary to retrace one's steps in order to make a better start. It may be necessary not merely to amend the covenant of the League, but to

[15] How far we are from any such conception of the relation of people to people is evident in the discussions that have taken place as to the vanquished people of Germany. The English Prime Minister, at one time, compared the German people to an animal whose back had been broken, writhing on the ground in convulsive agony, and therefore harmless. The dismemberment, the complete ruin of Germany, has been contemplated by some. And the most humane point of view that has since been reached is that the debtor nation should be suffi-

ciently restored to economic efficiency to meet its obligations to the victors, and to buy and sell under proper restrictions in the world market. That Germany, with all its errors and crimes (should not one rather say the crimes of its rulers?) has been a spiritual asset of the human race; that out of the mind and heart of this people, as out of a deep fountain, have come vast contributions to science and to the arts; that together with the Greeks and the Hindus, the Germans have been one of the chief philosophic peoples of the world, the originators of great philosophical systems, that they have advanced the scicnce and art of education—all this seems to have been forgotten. The one matter present to the minds of their neighbor nations is: Can they be made to pay, to buy? And the other question: Should the fountain that has flowed so generously in the past be choked up, or should it be helped to give forth life more purely? is scarcely asked. International love, if it existed, would teach a different attitude.

[16] In presenting the ideal of a perfect civilization as the aim of mankind, I have not in view an ethical millennium. It is the creative energy expended in rising to ever higher levels of achievement, and never the actual accomplishment itself, in

[8] Not because they fear to die (Lucretius's admonitions in this regard would be superfluous for most modern men), but because of their, intense bent toward activity, on which account they are averse to thinking of the moment when their activity must cease.

www.ingramcontent.com/pod-product-compliance
Lightning Source LLC
LaVergne TN
LVHW051627080426
835511LV00016B/2212